TH
SUTTA-NIPĀTA

THE SUTTA-NIPĀTA

Translated by

H. Saddhatissa

CURZON

First published in 1985

Published in 1994 by
Curzon Press
15 The Quadrant, Richmond
Surrey, TW9 1BP

Reprinted 1998

British Library Catalogue in Publication Data
A CIP catalogue record for this book
is available from the British Library

Library of Congress Cataloguing in Publication Data
A catalogue record for this book has been requested

Printed in Great Britain by
TJ International, Padstow, Cornwall

ISBN 0–7007–0181–8

CONTENTS

PREFACE

Only a handful of translations of the Sutta-Nipāta have been made in English but these are, doubtless because of their metrical rendering, generally archaic and stilted in expression; moreover, they are out of print.

I was persuaded to prepare a prose version which would convey the spirit of this important text in contemporary language and, it is hoped, stand the test of time more effectively than its predecessors. The present version is, therefore, presented for the consideration of readers who may find traditional interpretations inhibiting.

During my time at the universities of Benares (India) and Toronto (Canada) I taught the Sutta-Nipāta to undergraduates there. It was at this period that I began the first draft of this work, the first four chapters of which have been serialized in *Buddhist Quarterly* (now *Buddhist Forum*) the journal of the British Mahābodhi Society. It should be understood that it is not a strict translation but rather a rendering of the spirit of the *suttas*. In particular, I have abbreviated where there are frequent repetitions in the original.

In this task I must express indebtedness to three friends who polished the language and helped prepare the final manuscript: Robert Barnett (grandson of the late L.D. Barnett, Professor of Sanskrit in the University of London and Keeper of Oriental Printed Books at the British Museum); Dr P.D. Premasiri of the Department of Philosophy, University of Peradeniya (Sri Lanka); and Russell Webb (Honorary Secretary of the British Mahābodhi Society, London Buddhist Vihara).

London, September 1985 H. SADDHĀTISSA

INTRODUCTION

The canonical texts of the Theravādin school of Buddhism (the predominant religious tradition of South-East Asia and well represented in the West), collectively known as the Pali Canon, are divided into three main sections: Vinaya (the disciplinary rules and procedures governing the behaviour and daily life of the monks), Sutta (the discourses of the Buddha or his foremost ordained disciples addressed to both monks and lay followers) and Abhidhamma (the developed psychological writings which are generally acknowledged to post-date the historical Buddha's lifetime, *c.*560 – *c.*480 B.C.). All these texts were transmitted orally and only committed to ola leaf manuscripts in modern Sri Lanka (ancient Ceylon) in the first century B.C.

The collection of *suttas* is, in turn, sub-divided into five sections:
Dīgha Nikāya — which comprises long, mainly narrative discourses.
Majjhima Nikāya — medium length discourses which are generally regarded as the most important from the standpoint of the practical application of the Dhamma (or Doctrine/Teaching of the Buddha).
Saṃyutta Nikāya — detailed Dhamma prescriptions arranged in subject order.
Aṅguttara Nikāya — compressed narrative discourses which expound the Dhamma in numerical sequences.
Khuddaka Nikāya — which comprises fifteen individual books of which the best known is the Dhammapada (in over thirty English translations) and one of the most formative and influential, the Sutta-Nipāta.

Vernacular translations from Pali (the common tongue related to a Prakrit language in which the Buddha was reputed to use) as opposed to Sanskrit, the one-time preserve of the Indian brahmins, have been produced in Indian and South-East Asian languages and, during the last 150 years, Japanese and European languages. However, it is only in English that the Canon has appeared almost in its entirety, due primarily to the efforts of the Pali Text Society (f.1881) which is currently arranging for the complete translation of the traditional Commentaries.

Despite the foregoing, no completely lucid English translation of the Sutta-Nipāta has been made. A number of analytical studies have been produced by Pali scholars who have carefully examined the text's linguistic and historical features and its place in the Canon.

From such researches we can recognize four stages of literary development:

The (philosophical) Ascetic stage
The (disciplinary) Monastic stage
The (religious) Moralistic stage
The (commentarial) 'Legendary' stage

The first stage, embodied by the oldest strata of the Sutta-Nipāta (i.e. I 3, IV and V), was represented by the Buddha and his fellow 'homeless ones' who led an eremitic existence. His teaching was austere and stoical so as to lead to steadfastness of purpose and endeavour which would culminate in the final release from the unsatisfactoriness of mundane life — the mental state of Nibbāna (Nirvāna) — which could (and can) be attained here and now. Moderation and self-control were extolled; desire, prejudice and ill-will were repudiated; traditionalism was eschewed, despised, and rigid rules were regarded as fetters, as hindrances to that personal liberty of the spirit which is the hall mark of permanent Deliverance.

The specific text under consideration combines numerous features which make for a timeless and wider appeal than has hitherto been allowed for it: an analysis of psychological motivations which provides a refreshingly modern insight into human nature; an emphasis on *mental* detachment from the distractions of life; empirically-orientated philosophy which is subject to verifiable realization; fundamental doctrines of the Dhamma presented in a non-scholastic, unsystematized form; rationally-based exhortations to lead a balanced, ethical life; biographical sketches of the *Light of Asia* and vignettes of daily life in ancient India. All these features are couched in dialogue form, narrative prose or devotional verse, devoid of pedantry, niggling rules and regulations, repetitive or stereotyped stock formulae which appear elsewhere in later strata of the canonical texts.

The whole text conveys an atmosphere untrammelled by inhibiting conventions and with an emphasis on positive striving towards the desired goals of spiritual freedom and non-attachment. With its direct appeal to individual effort and self-discovery, as opposed to current commercialized and populist blandishments, this straightforward didactic work has a particular relevance today when a new generation is seeking a practical path leading to a purposeful life.

The numbers in parenthesis at the right of each verse correspond with the consecutive numbers of the stanzas as they appeared in the original text.

LIST OF SUTTAS

I. URAGAVAGGA	THE CHAPTER OF THE SNAKE
1. Uraga Sutta	The Snake's Skin
2. Dhaniya Sutta	Dhaniya the Herdsman
3. Khaggavisāṇa Sutta	The Unicorn's Horn
4. Kasībhāradvāja Sutta	The farmer Bhāradvāja
5. Cunda Sutta	Cunda the Smith
6. Parābhava Sutta	Downfall
7. Vasala Sutta	The Outcast
8. Mettā Sutta	Loving-kindness
9. Hemavata Sutta	Sātāgira and Hemavata
10. Āḷavaka Sutta	Āḷavaka
11. Vijaya Sutta	Victory over Delusion
12. Muni Sutta	The Sage

II. CŪLAVAGGA	THE MINOR CHAPTER
1. Ratana Sutta	Jewels
2. Āmagandha Sutta	Stench
3. Hiri Sutta	Shame
4. Mahāmangala Sutta	The Auspicious Performance
5. Sūciloma Sutta	Sūciloma
6. Dhammacariya Sutta	The Good Life
7. Brāhmaṇadhammika Sutta	The Good Conduct of the Brahmin
8. Nāvā Sutta	The Boat
9. Kiṃsīla Sutta	Right Conduct
10. Uṭṭhāna Sutta	Arousing
11. Rāhula Sutta	Rāhula
12. Vaṅgīsa Sutta	Vaṅgīsa
13. Sammāparibbājaniya Sutta	The Correct Homeless Life
14. Dhammika Sutta	Dhammika

III. MAHĀVAGGA	THE GREAT CHAPTER
1. Pabbajjā Sutta	The Going Forth
2. Padhāna Sutta	The Striving
3. Subhāsita Sutta	Good Words
4. Pūraḷāsa Sutta	The Sacrificial Cake
5. Māgha Sutta	Māgha
6. Sabhiya Sutta	Sabhiya
7. Sela Sutta	Sela

I. The Chapter of the Snake

1. URAGA SUTTA

The Snake's Skin

The monk who discards all human passions is compared to a snake that casts its skin

1 He who gives up anger which has arisen, as the snake poison diffused in the body is removed by antidotes, that monk gives up the Cycle of Existence as the snake sheds its old, decayed skin.[1] (1)

2 He who has completely destroyed lust as one cuts off a lotus flower in a lake, that monk . . . (2)

3 He who has completely destroyed craving like drying up a once swiftly-flowing river . . .[2] (3)

4 He who has completely destroyed pride like a weak bridge of reeds swept away by a mighty flood . . . (4)

5 He who does not see any substantiality in forms of becoming as one does not find flowers on a fig tree . . . (5)

6 He who has no ill-temper within him and who has overcome all forms of becoming . . . (6)

7 He who has destroyed speculations, who is well-prepared without remainder . . . (7)

8 He who is neither restless nor indolent and who has overcome all such impediments . . . (8)

9 He who is neither restless nor indolent and knows that all in the world is unsubstantial . . . (9)

10 He who is neither restless nor indolent and knowing that all is unsubstantial, freed from greed . . . (10)

11 He who is neither restless nor indolent and knowing that all is unsubstantial, freed from lust . . . (11)

12 He who is neither restless nor indolent and knowing that all is unsubstantial, freed from anger . . . (12)

13 He who is neither restless nor indolent and knowing that all is unsubstantial, freed from delusion . . . (13)

14 He who has no unhealthy tendencies whatsoever and has completely destroyed the roots of evil . . . (14)

15 He who has no anxieties whatsoever which are the causes of entering this world . . . (15)

16 He who has no cravings whatsoever which cause attachment to becoming . . . (16)

17 He who has eradicated the five hindrances,[3] freed from confusion, having overcome doubts and sorrow . . . (17)

Notes

1 Each stanza ends with the refrain: 'that monk gives up the Cycle of Existence as a snake sheds its old, decayed skin.'

2 Second part of the stanza in the text appears as *saritaṃ sīghasaraṃ visosayitvā*, whereas the Commentary states: *saritaṃ gataṃ pavattaṃ, sīghasaraṃ, sīghagāminiṃ, saritaṃ sīghasaraṃ pi taṇhaṃ.*

The latter means 'the craving which flows quickly'. In similar stanzas, the second and fourth similes have been given in the second part. On the analogy of these two stanzas, therefore, I feel that the reading has been corrupt, even during the Commentary period. I would suggest that it reads as *saritaṃ sīghasaraṃ va sosayitvā* and have translated it accordingly.

3 Sensuality, ill-will, physical and mental laziness, restlessness and worry, scepticism.

2. DHANIYA SUTTA

Dhaniya the Herdsman

A dialogue between Dhaniya and the Buddha, the one rejoicing in his worldly security and the other in his spiritual freedom

Dhaniya was a herdsman who lived at the time when the Buddha was staying at Sāvatthi. It was the monsoon season, just before the onset of rain. He had built strong shelters for himself, his family and for the cattle on the bank of the River Mahī. The Buddha, however, realized that this family was in danger of being overwhelmed by the flood and appeared in the cattle-keeper's shelter just when he was rejoicing in his comfort and security:

1 Dhaniya: I have cooked my rice and milked the cows. I dwell with my people near the bank of the Mahī. My house is thatched, the fire is kindled. Therefore, rain, O cloud, if you like! (18)

2 The Buddha: I am free from anger, free from passion. I abide for the night near the bank of the river Mahī. My house [body] is uncovered, the fire of passion is extinguished. Therefore, rain, O cloud, if you like! (19)

3 Dhaniya: Gadflies and mosquitoes are not to be found. My meadows are abounding with grass on the marshy land. The cattle can endure the rain when it comes. Therefore, rain, O cloud, if you like! (20)

4 The Buddha: By me is made a well-constructed raft [path] . I have passed over the floods to Nibbāna. There is no further use of the raft. Therefore, rain, O cloud, if you like! (21)

5 Dhaniya: Gopi, my wife, is not wanton and is obedient to me. For a long time she has lived with me pleasantly. Of her, I do not hear any evil whatever. (22)

6 The Buddha: My mind is obedient and is free from passion. For a long time it has been trained and well subdued. So evil is not to be found in me. (23)

7 Dhaniya: I am self-employed and support myself. My sons are all healthy. About them I do not hear any evil whatever. (24)

8 The Buddha: I am no one's servant. With the gaining of my object [Buddhahood] I wander through the world; there is no need for me to serve. (25)

9 Dhaniya: I have young bulls and calves, also cows in calf and heifers, and a bull who is leader of the herd. (26)

10 The Buddha: I have neither young bulls nor calves, neither cows in calf nor heifers, nor a bull who is leader of the herd. (27)

11 Dhaniya: The stakes are firmly fixed. The ropes made of muñja grass are new and well made. Even the young calves are not able to break them. (28)

12 The Buddha: Having broken the fetters like a bull, as an elephant having broken the pūtilatā creepers, so there will be no more rebirth for me. (29)

13 (Then all of a sudden a shower poured down, filling all the levels and hollows. Hearing the roaring of the storm Dhaniya spoke the following words:) (30)

14 Great, indeed is the gain that we see the Blessed one, the Omniscient One, to you we come for refuge, O Great Seer, be our refuge! (31)

15 Both my wife and I will be obedient to you in the dispensation of Sugata, the Welcome One. We shall lead the Holy Life; overcoming birth and death we will make an end of suffering. (32)

16 Māra[1] now appeared to tempt him: He who has children delights on account of the children. He who has cattle likewise delights on account of cattle. For the delights of man are on account of elements of sensory existence (*upadhi*) alone. He who has no *upadhi* has no delight. (33)

17 The Buddha: He who has children has grief on account of his children. He who has cattle has grief on account of cattle. For *upadhi* is the cause of the sorrows of men, but he who has no *upadhi* has no sorrow. (34)

Note

1 *Māra* literally means 'the killer' or 'bringer of death'. In Buddhist literature 'passion', 'anger', 'temptation', 'temper' or 'evils' have been personified as Māra (the Evil One). From the time of the Buddha's enlightenment until his *parinibbāna*, Māra made his appearance on various occasions assuming divine, human or even animal forms. According to Buddhist literature there are five kinds of Māra: (i) the five aggregates, (ii) kammic activities, (iii) death, (iv) mental defilements, and (v) a deity. In this instance the term is used in the sense of 'passion' or 'evils' personified. His army consists of ten forces: (i) sense desire, (ii) discontent, (iii) hunger and thirst, (iv) craving, (v) lethargy and drowsiness, (vi) cowardice, (vii) uncertainty, (viii) distraction and obstinacy, (ix) gain, praise, honour and undeserved fame, and (x) the extolling of oneself whilst disparaging others.

3. KHAGGAVISĀṆA SUTTA

The Unicorn's Horn

Sensory attachment and association with others should be avoided

1 Having abandoned the harming of living beings, not tormenting even one of them, let one not wish for a son, not to speak of a friend! Let one live alone like a unicorn's horn.[1] (35)

2 Attachment arises from companionship, dissatisfaction proceeds from attachment, observing the perils resulting from attachment . . . (36)

3 Being compassionate to friends and dear ones, having a fettered heart, he neglects the general welfare seeing such fear in intimacy . . . (37)

4 The attachment towards children and wives is like a bamboo clump thickly grown and entangled. Being, therefore, free from entanglement like the new bamboo tip . . . (38)

5 Like the unfettered forest deer, roaming and feeding at leisure, let the wise man observing his freedom live alone . . . (39)

6 One is petitioned with requests if he is among friends, during rest, whilst being entertained, whilst on a visit or during a journey. Observing the freedom that is not desired by others . . . (40)

7 Love of amusement and desire arises in the midst of friends and also arises strong attachment for children. Loathing the conditions for separation from beloved ones . . . (41)

8 One who has no hatred towards any of the four directions, being contented with little or much, having overcome all danger, fearless . . . (42)

9 Some monks are difficult to please, also the laity living the household life. Having become unconcerned about other's children . . . (43)

10 Having given up the characteristics of a layman like the Kovilāra tree[2] which has cast off its leaves, having broken the fetters of the household life, the courageous one lives alone . . . (44)

11 If one finds a wise friend, a companion living according to good virtues, prudent and having conquered all dangers, then live with him happily and mindfully. (45)

12 If one does not find a wise friend, a companion living according to good virtues, and prudent, then like a ruler who has abandoned his conquered country . . . (46)

13 Certainly we praise the acquisition of friendship and friends — those who are either higher or equal in attainment or development should be associated with. Not finding such friends enjoying blameless food[3] . . . (47)

14 Having seen the glittering golden armlets well finished by the goldsmith which strike against each other on one's arm . . . (48)

15 Thus, 'When I live with a second person I am either compelled to speak too much or to be angry with him.' Observing these fears in the future . . . (49)

16 Sensuous objects are indeed varied, sweet and delightful, and upset the mind by their illusions. Seeing the unhealthy results of sensuous objects . . . (50)

17 'Sensuous objects are the cause of calamity, danger, disease, a dart and a fear to me.' Observing this danger resulting from sensuous objects . . . (51)

18 There are cold, heat, hunger, thirst, wind, sun, insects, snakes. Having endured all these things . . . (52)

19 Like the huge-bodied, white-marked noble elephant wandering in the forest to his heart's content, abandoning his herd . . . (53)

20 'Even temporary deliverance is impossible to the person who is fond of society.' Observing these words of Ādiccabandhu[4] . . . (54)

21 'I have removed wrong views, gained the right Path and indeed arrived at the end. Wisdom is born in me and I have understood with my own effort.' Let . . . (55)

22 Being free from greed and deceit, without craving and envy, having removed ignorance, having no desire for anything in the whole world . . . (56)

23 The cynical friend who indulges in mischief, who is attached to wrong views, is to be avoided. Such a friend who is irresponsible should not be associated with . . . (57)

24 One should associate with a friend who is learned, who knows the doctrine, developed and possessed of knowledge, having known the meaning of things and removed his doubts . . . (58)

25 One who disdains sport, amusement and worldly pleasure, avoiding a life of self-aggrandisement, speaking the truth . . . (59)

26 Having abandoned the excessive desires with regard to son, wife, father, mother, wealth, tangible goods and relations . . .(60)

27 Attachment to things is a bond, here happiness is temporary and sorrow is greater and enjoyment is less. The wise person knowing this to be like a fish-hook in the throat lives alone . . . (61)

28 Having broken the ties like a fish which has broken the net in the river, like the fire that does not return to a burnt-up spot . . . (62)

29 With downcast eyes, not fond of loitering, with guarded sense and restrained mind which is not soaked by lust and is not burning with it . . . (63)

30 Having given up the sartorial characteristics of the householder like the Paricchatta[5] tree with leaves destroyed, having gone forth clad in yellow robes . . . (64)

31 Not greedy for delicacies, not disturbed by tastes, having no one dependent on him, begging from house to house without any attachment to those families . . . (65)

32 Having eliminated the five hindrances[6] from the mind, having destroyed all defilements of the mind, having broken the fetters of attachment and being free . . . (66)

33 Doing away with happiness and sorrow and the previous mental ease and mental agony, having gained equanimity, calm and purity . . . (67)

34 In order to attain the supreme good, being strenuous, prudent, industrious, resolute in perseverance, possessed of the power of strength . . . (68)

35 Not abandoning solitude and meditation, living always according to the Dhamma, realizing the painful consequences of forms of becoming . . . (69)

36 Being diligent, aspiring to the eradication of craving, skilled, learned, mindful, proficient to examine the Dhamma, sure in the Path, energetic . . . (70)

37 Like a lion not frightened by noises, like wind not in a net, like a lotus not smeared with the water . . . (71)

38 As a lion, the king of beasts, strong with his teeth, roams overcoming other beasts, living in solitary surroundings . . . (72)

39 Practising loving-kindness, equanimity, compassion, deliverance, and sympathetic joy at the appropriate time, unobstructed by all the world . . . (73)

40 Having discarded lust, anger and delusion, having broken the fetters,[7] entertaining no fear in death . . . (74)

41 Many keep companionship and associate with each other for the sake of self-advantage. Today, it is difficult to find friends free from ulterior motives. They are clever enough to obtain personal advantages and therefore are despicable. Knowing this, let . . . (75)

Notes

1 Some scholars have translated *khaggavisāṇākappa* as 'like the rhinoceros'. The Commentary suggests: *Ettha Khaggavisāṇaṃ nāma khaggavisāsiṅgaṃ. Khaggavisāṇakappo ti khaggavisāṇasadiso ti vuttaṃ hoti.* I have rendered it accordingly. Moreover, in view of the gregarious nature of the Indian species, called *Rhinoceros unicornis*, I have chosen the latter term to emphasize solitariness symbolically.

Each stanza, except 11, ends with the refrain: 'Let one live alone like a unicorn's horn.'

2 Kovilāra: *Bahunia variegata*, a kind of mountain ebony.

3 Food obtained by rightful means.

4 A Pacceka Buddha.

5 It is considered to be a tree in the Tāvatiṃsa heaven: See *Dictionary of Pāli Proper Names* 1, p. 191.

6 See note 3 on v.17 of the Uraga Sutta.

7 The ten fetters by which beings are bound to the wheel of existence: 1. self-delusion, 2. doubt, 3. clinging to rites and ceremonies, 4. sensual lust, 5. ill-will, 6. greed for material existence, 7. greed for immaterial existence, 8. conceit, 9. restlessness, 10. ignorance.

4. KASĪBHĀRADVĀJA SUTTA

The farmer Bhāradvāja

Kasībhāradvāja reproaches the Buddha with idleness but the latter convinces him that he also works

Thus have I heard: Once the Buddha was dwelling in a brahmin village called Ekanāḷā situated in the district of Dakkhiṇāgiri in the country of Magadha.

At that time, being the sowing season, five hundred ploughs owned by the brahmin Kasībhāradvāja were set to work. In the morning then, the Buddha, having robed himself and taking his bowl and (double-layered) robe, went to that place where Kasībhāradvāja's work was in progress. It was lunch time and the food was being distributed by the brahmin. When the Buddha arrived at the place where the food was being distributed he stood aside. The brahmin, seeing the Buddha standing for alms, said thus: 'O recluse, I plough and sow, and having ploughed and sown, I eat. You also, recluse, should plough and sow; and having ploughed and sown, you should eat.'

'I too, brahmin, plough and sow; and having ploughed and sown, I eat.'

'We see neither yoke, nor plough, nor ploughshare, nor goad, nor oxen of the Venerable Gotama, and yet you say: "I too, brahmin, plough and sow; and having ploughed and sown, I eat." ' There upon Kasībhāradvāja addressed the Buddha in this stanza:

1 'You claim to be a farmer, yet we do not see your ploughing. Being questioned by us about your ploughing, tell us in such a manner that we may know of it.' (76)

2 'Confidence is the seed; self-control the rein; wisdom my yoke and plough; modesty is my pole; mind is the rope; mindfulness my ploughshare and goad. (77)

3 'Bodily action is well-guarded, speech is well-guarded, moderate in food, I make truth the destroyer of weeds and calm my release. (78)

4 'Exertion is my yoked-oxen which carries me towards Nibbāna. It goes onward without stopping; having gone there one has no regrets. (79)

5 'In this way the ploughing is done; it bears the fruit of immortality. Having accomplished this ploughing, one becomes free from all suffering.' (80)

Then Kasībhāradvāja filled a large golden bowl with milk-rice and offered it to the Buddha, saying: 'Let the Venerable Gotama eat the milk-rice. You are a farmer by reason of that ploughing; it bears indeed the fruit of immortality.'

6 'What is obtained by chanting hymns is not to be eaten by me. This is, brahmin, not the practice of those who see rightly. The Buddhas refuse what is obtained by chanting hymns. (81)

7 'You should serve other food and drink to an accomplished great sage who is free from the mental impurities and remorse. That is the field for him who seeks merits.' (82)

'Then, Venerable Gotama, to whom should I give this milk-rice?'

'Brahmin, in the world which includes gods, Māras, Brahmas, and among brahmins and men I do not see anyone except a Tathāgata[1] or a disciple of a Tathāgata, by whom this milk-rice, when eaten, can be properly digested.

'Therefore, O brahmin, you had better cast this milk-rice either in a place where there is no grass or float it in water where there are no living creatures.'

So Kasībhāradvāja floated the milk-rice in water which contained no life whereupon it made a hissing sound with much steam and smoke emanating from all sides, just as a ploughshare when heated all day and plunged into water produces a hissing sound and emits steam and smoke on all sides.

Then Kasībhāradvāja, greatly excited and with hair standing on end, approached the Buddha and fell with his head at the Master's feet, saying: 'It is amazing, Venerable Gotama, it is wonderful, Venerable Gotama! Just as if one might raise what has been overturned, or reveal what has been hidden, or point out the way to him who has gone astray, or hold out a lamp in the dark so that those who have eyes may see objects, so likewise has the Truth been explained by Venerable Gotama in various ways. Therefore, I take refuge in him, his Dhamma and his Sangha.[2] I wish to enter the homeless life and to receive the higher ordination near the Venerable Gotama.'

Then Kasībhāradvāja received ordination as a novice and received the higher ordination near the Buddha.

Later, by leading a secluded life, diligently, energetically and with a resolute will, in a short time he understood, experienced and attained that highest perfection of a noble life for which the sons of good families leave the household life, harmoniously and take to the life of homelessness. Rebirth had been ended; a noble life had been led; what was to be done had been done and there was nothing else to be done in this earthly existence: Kasībhāradvāja had become one of the arahants [perfected ones].

Notes

1 The term used by the Buddha when referring to himself. For details see H. Saddhatissa *Buddhist Ethics*, George Allen & Unwin, London 1970, p. 33.

2 Community of monks. See *Buddhist Ethics*, pp. 79f.

5. CUNDA SUTTA

Cunda the Smith

The Buddha describes the four kinds of monks

1 Cunda: I ask the sage Buddha of great wisdom, Lord of Dhamma, who is free from craving, the noblest of men, the noblest of guides; how many kinds of monks are there in the world? Please tell me. (83)

2 The Buddha: Cunda, there are four kinds of monks, not a fifth. I shall elucidate them to you, since you ask me: (i) one kind has won the Path, (ii) one expounds the Path, (iii) one lives on the Path, and (iv) one defiles the Path. (84)

3 Cunda: Whom does the Buddha describe as one who has won the Path? How does the one who expounds the Path become incomparable? Tell me about the one who lives on the Path and then explain to me the one who defiles the Path. (85)

4 The Buddha: One who overcomes uncertainty, is freed from sorrow, delights in Nibbāna, is detached, a guide of men and gods — such a person is said by the Buddhas to be one who has won the Path. (86)

5 Here, one knows Nibbāna as the noblest (state) and expounds and explains the Dhamma; that sage who destroys uncertainty, is desireless — this second of monks is called the one who expounds the Path. (87)

6 One who has controlled himself mindfully, lives well on the Path according to the words of Dhamma well expounded; one who practises correct principles — this third of monks is called the one who lives on the Path. (88)

7 One who disguises himself by wearing the robes of the well-conducted ones, travels for gain, disgraces families, is impudent, deceitful, unrestrained, a gossip and waffler pretending to be a real monk — he is one who defiles the Path. (89)

8 Having comprehended these (four) he who is well-versed, house-holder, who is a noble, wise disciple and who has understood that 'all of them are not alike'; seeing thus, he does not diminish his confidence. How could the defiled one and the undefiled one, the pure and the impure one, be considered as equals? (90)

6. PARĀBHAVA SUTTA

Downfall

A dialogue between a deity and the Buddha on the causes of spiritual decline

Thus have I heard: Once the Buddha was living near Sāvatthi in the Jeta Grove at Anāthapiṇḍika's monastery. Then, one beautiful night, a certain devatā, having illuminated the whole Jeta Grove with surpassing splendour, came to the Buddha and, making salutations, stood on one side and uttered these words:

1 I wish to ask you, Gotama, about a person who suffers downfall. I have approached you in order to inquire as to the causes of downfall. (91)

The Buddha:

2 Easily known is the progressive one, easily known the one who declines. He who loves Dhamma progresses, he who hates it declines. (92)[1]

4 One who loves the company of the vicious finds no delight with the virtuous; he prefers the doctrine of the vicious — this is a cause of one's downfall. (94)

6 Being fond of sleep, talkative, lethargic, lazy and irritable — this is a cause of one's downfall. (96)

8 He who being sufficiently affluent does not support his father and mother who are old and infirm — this is a cause of one's downfall. (98)

10 He who deceives by falsehood a priest, monk or any other spiritual preceptor — this is the cause of one's downfall. (100)

12 Having ample wealth, assets and property, enjoying them alone — this is a cause of one's downfall. (102)

14 If a man is conceited through his birth, wealth or community and looks down on his own kith and kin — this is a cause of one's downfall. (104)

16 To be a womaniser, a drunkard, a gambler, and to squander all one earns — this is a cause of one's downfall. (106)

18 Not to be contented with one's wife but to be seen with a prostitute or the wives of others — this is a cause of one's downfall. (108)

20 Being past one's youth, to take a young wife and to be unable to sleep for jealousy of her — this is a cause of one's downfall. (110)

22 To place in authority a woman given to drink and squandering, or a man of like behaviour — this is a cause of one's downfall. (112)

24 If a member of an influential family [or social or other grouping], with vast ambition and of slender means, seeks power or control over others — this is a cause of one's downfall. (114)

25 Reflecting thoroughly on those causes of downfall in the world, the wise one, endowed with insight, enjoys bliss in a happy state. (115)

Notes

1 The questioning stanzas — 93, 95, 97, 99, 101, 103, 105, 107, 109, 111 and 113 — have been omitted.

7. VASALA SUTTA[1]

The Outcast

The Buddha's definition of a (spiritual) outcast

Thus have I heard: Once the Buddha was living near Sāvatthi in the Jeta Grove at Anāthapiṇḍika's monastery. Then, in the forenoon, having robed himself and taking his bowl, he entered Sāvatthi for alms. At that time, in the house of the Brahmin Aggika-Bhāradvāja, the fire-worshipper, a fire was lit and the objects for sacrifice were made ready.

Then the Buddha, going from house to house, came to that brahmin's abode. Seeing the Buddha approaching he shouted: 'Stop there, shaveling, stop there, ascetic, stop there, outcast!'

The Buddha (calmly replied): 'O brahmin, can you recognize an outcast or know those things that constitute an outcast?'

'No, indeed, Master Gotama, I cannot recognize an outcast or know those things that constitute an outcast. It would be profitable, therefore, Master Gotama, if you were to enlighten me on this matter'.

The Buddha (continued): 'Very well, brahmin, listen and bear well in your mind what follows:

1 Whoever is angry, harbours ill-will, is evil-minded and envious; whose views are delusive, who is deceitful, he is to be known as an outcast.[2] (116)

2 Whoever destroys life, whether bird or animal, insect or fish, has no compassion for life . . . (117)

3 Whoever is destructive or aggressive in town and country and is a known vandal or thug . . . (118)

4 Whoever steals what is considered to belong to others, whether it be situated in villages or the forest . . . (119)

5 Whoever having contracted debts defaults when asked to pay, retorts, 'I am *not* indebted to you!' . . . (120)

6 Whoever is desirous of stealing even a trifle and takes such a thing, having killed a man going along the road[3] . . . (121)

7 Whoever commits perjury either for his own benefit, for that of others or for the sake of profit . . . (122)

8 Whoever has illicit affairs with the wives of his relatives or friends, either by force or through mutual consent . . . (123)

9 Whoever does not support his father or mother, who are old and infirm, being himself in a prosperous position . . . (124)

10 Whoever strikes or abuses by words either father, mother, brother, sister or mother-in-law . . . (125)

11 Whoever being asked for good advice teaches what is misleading or speaks in obscure terms . . . (126)

12 Whoever having committed an offence wishes to conceal it from others and is a hypocrite . . . (127)

13 Whoever having gone to another's house and taken advantage of the hospitality there does not reciprocate in like manner. . . (128)

14 Whoever deceives a priest, monk or any other spiritual preceptor . . . (129)

15 Whoever abuses by words and does not serve a priest or monk coming for a meal . . . (130)

16 Whoever, being enmeshed in ignorance, makes untrue predictions for paltry gain . . . (131)

17 Whoever exalts himself and despises others, smug in his self-conceit . . . (132)

18 Whoever is a provoker (of quarrels) or is avaricious, has malicious desires, is envious, shameless and has no qualms in committing evil . . . (133)

19 Whoever insults the Buddha or his disciples, whether renounced ones or laymen . . . (134)

20 Whoever not being an arahant pretends to be one, he is indeed the greatest rogue in the whole world, the lowest outcast of all. Thus have I exposed those who are outcasts. (135)

21 One does not become an outcast by birth, one does not become a brahmin by birth. It is by deed that one becomes an outcast, it is by deed that one becomes a brahmin. (136)

22 Now listen and I will give you an illustration. Once there was the son of an outcast whose name was Mātaṅga of the Sopāka caste. (137)

23 He attained the pinnacle of fame and when he had done so, warriors, brahmins and many others came to serve him. (138)

24 Having destroyed worldly passions, he entered that Noble Path and reached the Brahmā world. Caste did not prevent him from being born in the heavenly realm. (139)

25 Those brahmins who are familiar with the Vedas and who are born in a family which recites the Vedas, if they are addicted to evil deeds, (140)

26 They are not only disgraced in this life itself but in the next they are born in a state of suffering. Caste does not prevent them from disgrace or birth in a painful state.' (141)

27 (Here, v.21 is repeated) (142)

When the Buddha had spoken, the brahmin Aggika-Brāradvāja exclaimed: 'It is amazing, Venerable Gotama, it is wonderful, Venerable Gotama! Just as if one might raise what has been overturned, or reveal what has been hidden, or point out the way to him who has gone astray, or hold out a lamp in the dark so that those who have eyes may see objects, so likewise has the Truth been explained by Venerable Gotama in various ways. Therefore, I take refuge in him, his Dhamma and his Sangha. May the Venerable Gotama accept me as a lay follower who henceforth has taken refuge in him for the rest of his life!'

Notes

1 Also called the *Aggika-Bhāradvāja Sutta*.
2 From 2 to 19 each stanza ends with the refrain, 'he is to be known as an outcast.'
3 The earliest reference to 'mugging'?

8. METTA SUTTA

Loving-kindness

In praise of love and goodwill towards all beings

1 He who is skilled in welfare, who wishes to attain that calm state [Nibbāna], should act thus: he should be able, upright, perfectly upright, of noble speech, gentle and humble. (143)

2 Contented, easily supported, with few duties, of light livelihood, with senses calmed, discreet, not impudent, not greedily attached to families. (144)

3 He should not pursue the slightest thing for which otherwise men might censure him. May all beings be happy and secure, may their hearts be wholesome! (145)

4 – 5 Whatever living beings there be: feeble or strong, tall, stout or medium, short, small or large, without exception; seen or unseen, those dwelling far or near, those who are born or those who are to be born, may all beings be happy! (146 – 7)

6 Let none deceive another, not despise any person whatsoever in any place. Let him not wish any harm to another out of anger or ill-will. (148)

7 Just as a mother would protect her only child at the risk of her own life, even so, let him cultivate a boundless heart towards all beings. (149)

8 Let his thoughts of boundless love pervade the whole world: above, below and across without any obstruction, without any hatred, without any enmity. (150)

9 Whether he stands, walks, sits or lies down, as long as he is awake, he should develop this mindfulness. This they say is the noblest living here. (151)

10 Not falling into wrong views, being virtuous and endowed with insight, by discarding attachment to sense desires, never again is he reborn. (152)

9. HEMAVATA SUTTA

Sātāgira and Hemavata

A dialogue between two demons on the qualities of the Buddha — and after having their questions answered they become his followers

1 The yakkha Sātāgira says: Today is the full moon day of the lunar month. The divine night has approached. Let's see Master Gotama, the teacher of perfect name. (153)

2 The yakkha Hemavata says: Is the steadfast one's mind well directed towards all beings? Has he brought his thoughts as regards pleasant and unpleasant things under his control? (154)

3 Sātāgira: The steadfast one's mind is well directed towards all beings. Moreover, he has brought his thoughts as regards pleasant and unpleasant things under his control. (155)

4 Hemavata: Does he not steal? Is he self-controlled towards living beings? Is he far from being lethargic? Does he not give up meditation? (156)

5 Sātāgira: He does not steal. His attitude is one of self-control towards living beings. He is far from being lethargic. The Enlightened One does not abandon meditation. (157)

6 Hemavata: Does he not speak falsehood? Does he not use harsh words? Does he not say things which cause distress? Does he not indulge in frivolous talk? (158)

7 Sātāgira: He does not speak falsehood. Neither does he use harsh words nor does he say things which cause distress. He speaks [only] wise and useful things. (159)

8 Hemavata: Is he not attached to worldly pleasures? Is his mind undisturbed? Has he overcome delusion? Has he acquired insight into all things? (160)

9 Sātāgira: He is not attached to worldly pleasures. His mind is undisturbed? All his delusion has vanished. The Enlightened One possesses insight into all things. (161)

10 Hemavata: Is he endowed with knowledge? Is his conduct pure? Has he destroyed all passions? Has be brought to an end [the cycle of] rebirth? (162)

11 Sātāgira: He is endowed with knowledge. His conduct is pure. He has destroyed all passions. He will not be subject to [further] rebirth. (163)

12 Hemavata: The sage's mind is filled with good speech and action. He possesses right knowledge and conduct. Let's go and see Gotama! (164)

13 The sage Gotama, limbed like the antelope, lean, firm, taking little food, not greedy, who meditates in the jungle. Let's go and see him! (165)

14 Having approached him, who is like a lion, who lives alone, who is indifferent to worldly pleasures, let's ask for an escape from the snare of death. (166)

15 [Both speak] We ask Gotama, the Englightened One, who declares the Dhamma, who expounds the Dhamma, who has realized all truth, who has overcome hatred and fear. (167)

16 Hemavata: Upon what is the world produced? With what is the world intimate; After having clung to what by what is the world troubled? (168)

17 The Buddha: O Hemavata, in six is the world produced, with six is it intimate, after having clung to six by six the world is troubled. (169)

18 Hemavata: What is that attachment by which the world is troubled? Please tell us the [means of] deliverance; how does the world escape from misery? (170)

19 The Buddha: Having destroyed the desire of the five sensual pleasures in the world, and that of mind, the sixth sense, one escapes from misery. (171)

20 This is the salvation of the world — I have told you as it is. This alone I tell you: thus the world escapes from misery. (172)

21 Hemavata: Who is the one who crosses the flood? Who is the one who crosses the sea? Without a footing, and when not supported, who will not sink in the deep ocean and sea? (173)

22 The Buddha: One who is always virtuous, wise, well concentrated, reflects within himself, and mindful, he crosses the flood which is difficult to cross. (174)

23 Abstaining from lustful thoughts and having broken all fetters, being one in whom desire for existence is extinct, he will not sink into the deep. (175)

24 Hemavata: Look at that great sage who possesses deep wisdom, who is subtle in realizing the truth, passionless, not attached to worldly pleasures, free from all fetters and who walks on the superhuman Path! (176)

25 Look at that great sage of perfect name, who is subtle in realizing the truth, who imparts wisdom, who is not attached to worldly pleasures, who is all knowing, whose wisdom is perfect, who walks on the noble Path! (177)

26 A good sight indeed has arisen today, a good daybreak, a beautiful arising, for we have seen the perfectly Enlightened One, who has crossed the flood, who is free from passions. (178)

27 These thousand spirits assembled here who possess supernatural power and fame all take refuge in you. You are our noble teacher. (179)

28 Thus we shall wander from village to village and mountain to mountain paying our respects to the Enlightened One and to his doctrine which is well preached. (180)

10. ĀḶAVAKA SUTTA

Āḷavaka

Another demon first threatens the Buddha and then puts some questions to him which are answered

Thus have I heard: Once the Buddha was dwelling in the residence of the yakkha Āḷavaka near the town of Āḷavi. Then Āḷavaka came to the Buddha and shouted: 'Get out, recluse!' The Buddha departed, saying: 'Very well, friend.' The yakkha then ordered: 'Come in, recluse!' Saying, 'Yes, friend', the Buddha entered. For a second time the yakkha shouted thus to the Buddha: 'Get out, recluse!' The Buddha again departed, saying 'Very well, friend.' For a second time the yakkha ordered: 'Come in, recluse!' Saying, 'Yes, friend', the Buddha again entered. For a third time also the yakkha shouted: 'Get out, recluse!' And for a third time the Buddha departed, saying 'Very well, friend'. However, when Āḷavaka shouted his orders to the Buddha yet again the Buddha retorted: 'I will not obey you and you can do whatever you like about it!' 'I shall put a question to you then, recluse, and if you do not answer I will pervert your mind or tear out your heart or take you by the feet and throw you to the other side of the river!' 'I do not see, friend, in the world of gods, Māras, Brahmas, or men anyone who could do to me such as you say. However, friend, proceed with your question.'

1 Āḷavaka: What is the best wealth to a man in this world? What is the good practice that brings happiness? What is the sweetest of all tastes? What manner of living is said to be the noblest kind? (181)

2 The Buddha: Confidence is the best wealth to a man in this world. Well practised Dhamma brings [the most] happiness. Truth is the sweetest of all tastes. Living with wisdom is said to be the noblest kind. (182)

3 Āḷavaka: How does one cross the flood [of recurrent birth]? How does one cross the sea [of existence]? How does one transcend unhappiness? How does one get purified? (183)

4 The Buddha: One crosses the flood [of cycles of birth and death = *Samsāra*] by confidence. One crosses the sea [of existence] by vigilance. One transcends unhappiness by strenuous effort. One purifies oneself by wisdom. (184)

5 Āḷavaka: How does one acquire knowledge? How does one obtain wealth? How does one attain fame? How does one gain friends? How does one not repent passing from this world to the next? (185)

6 The Buddha: One acquires knowledge by reposing confidence and listening to the Dhamma of the arahants for the attainment of Nibbāna, being diligent and attentive. (186)

7 One who does what is proper, one who is resolute, one who is industrious acquires wealth. One attains fame by truth. One who gives gains friends. (187)

8 The confident householder in whom there are four virtues — truthfulness, goodness, energy and generosity — will not repent after his death. (188)

9 I challenge you to consult other ascetics and brahmins to ascertain whether there can be any other qualities higher than truth, self-control, generosity and patience! (189)

10 Āḷavaka: Why should I consult other ascetics and brahmins? Today I know which one will prove for my good in the future. (190)

11 The Buddha, indeed, came to my residence near Āḷavi for my benefit! Today I know what should be given to achieve great results. (191)

12 From today I will wander from village to village, from town to town, paying my respects to the Fully Enlightened One and to his perfect teaching! (192)

11. VIJAYA[1] SUTTA

Victory over Delusion

A reflection on the unattractive nature of the human body

1 Anyone, either walking, standing, sitting or lying down, contracts or stretches his body — such is the motion of the body. (193)

2 The body is put together with bones and sinews, plastered with skin and flesh whose real nature is not perceived. (194)

3 It is filled with intestines in the stomach, the lump of the liver in the abdomen, the bladder, heart, lungs, kidneys and spleen; (195)

4 With mucus, saliva, perspiration, lymph, blood, the synovial fluid, bile and fat. (196)

5 Then in nine streams impurity constantly oozes — from the eye conjunctivitis, from the ear otitis; (197)

6 From the nose mucus; sometimes the body emits vomit from the mouth and ejects bile and phlegm; from the body comes sweat and dirt. (198)

7 The cavity of the head is filled with the brain; but the fool, because of his ignorance, regards it as a fine thing; (199)

8 When the body lies dead, swollen and livid, cast away in the cemetery, the relatives do not care for it. (200)

9 Dogs, jackals, wolves, worms, crows and vultures and other living creatures eat it. (201)

10 In the world, the monk who is wise, listening to the Buddha's word, fully comprehends the body and sees it in its true perspective. (202)

11 He compares his body to a corpse and thinking that this body is the same as a corpse and a corpse the same as this body, he removes desire for his own body. (203)

12 In the world, such a wise monk who is freed from desire and attachment attains the immortal, tranquil and deathless state of Nibbāna. (204)

13 The body is impure, bad-smelling and replete with various kinds of stench which trickle here and there. (205)

14 If one, possessed of such a body, thinks highly of himself and despises others — that is due to nothing other than his lack of insight. (206)

Note

1 *Vijaya* or 'victory'. Here, 'victory' over the delusion concerning the body-frame of impurities. This sutta is also called the *Kāyavicchandanika Sutta*, the discourse on the unattractive nature of the body.

12. MUNI[1] SUTTA

The Sage

In praise of the solitary life of self-control

1 Fear arises because of intimacy. Sensual desire is born of the household life. Homelessness and detachment is, therefore, appreciated by the sage. (207)

2 One who cuts off defilements that have arisen, who would not plant them again and who would not enter into what is being grown, he is said to be the solitary wandering sage. That great sage has seen the State of Peace [Nibbāna]. (208)

3 Having considered the ground, having discarded the seed and not supplying moisture for the growth of that seed; having abandoned sophistry, that sage who has seen the end of birth cannot be categorically described. (209)

4 He who has known all kinds of births, but does not desire to enter into any of them, such a sage is free from greed and desire; he toils not, for he has reached the Other Shore [Nibbāna]. (210)

5 One who has overcome all, who knows all, who is intelligent, who does not cling to any object, who has abandoned everything, who has freed himself by destroying desire, is called a sage by the wise. (211)

6 One who possesses the strength of wisdom, born of the moral precepts and restraints, who is tranquil in mind and delights in meditation, who is mindful, free from attachment, free from fallowness of mind and the Intoxicants,[2] is . . .[3] (212)

7 The sage who wanders alone, who is diligent and undisturbed by praise or blame, not frightened by noises — like a lion, not caught in a net — like the wind, not soiled by water — like the lotus, leading others but not led by others, is . . . (213)

8 One who is firm as the post in a bathing place, controlled over what others say, who is passionless, whose senses are well composed, is . . . (214)

9 One who is firm minded and straight as a shuttle, who despises evil actions, investigating what is good and bad, is . . . (215)

10 One who is self-restrained and does not commit evil, that wise one, whether young or middle-aged, whose mind is well restrained, who is not provoked and who does not provoke others, is . . . (216)

11 The monk who depends on others, who does not praise or blame the giver when he has received alms either from the top (portion), or the middle (portion), or the remainder and who neither flatters nor treats with disrespect, is . . . (217)

12 The sage who wanders alone, who has abstained from sexual intimacy, who even in his youth is not attached to anything, who has detached himself from pride and indolence, is . . . (218)

13 One who has known the world, who has perceived the highest truth, who has crossed the flood and sea [of existence], who has cut the ties [of rebirth], who has no clinging to sense-objects, who is free from the Intoxicants,[2] is . . . (219)

14 The sage who is accustomed to living in distant places, the egoless and well-conducted one and the householder who supports a family — they are not equal. For the householder is unrestrained and destroys living beings; the sage is self-restrained and protects living beings. (220)

15 The blue-necked peacock which flies through the air, never approaches the speed of the swan. Similarly, the householder can never resemble the monk who is endowed with the qualities of a sage who meditates, aloof, in the jungle. (221)

Notes

1 One who has made the vow of silence, a sage, a wise one. The term is applied to anyone who has attained to insight, self-restraint and perfection.

2 Intoxicants — *āsavas*: sense-desire (*kāmāsava*), desire for the process of life (*bhavāsava*), lack of higher knowledge or ignorance (*avijjāsava*), and views (*diṭṭhāsava*). See H. Saddhatissa *Buddhist Ethics, op. cit.*, p. 83, footnote 2.

3 From 6 to 13 each stanza ends with the refrain, 'is called a sage by the wise.'

II. The Minor Chapter

1. RATANA[1] SUTTA

Jewels

In praise of the 'jewels' of the Buddha, Dhamma and Sangha

1 Whatever beings are assembled here, whether terrestrial or celestial, let all such beings be happy; let them, moreover, attentively listen to what is said. (222)

2 Therefore, O beings, do you all pay attention; diffuse loving-kindness towards mankind who day and night bring offerings to you. Protect them, therefore, with earnestness. (223)

3 Whatever treasure there be either here or in the other world, or whatever precious jewel is in the heavenly worlds, yet there is none comparable with the Tathāgata. This precious jewel is in the Buddha. By this truth may there be peace! (224)

4 The sage of the Sākyas of a tranquil mind, realized that cessation which is passionless, immortal and excellent. There is nothing equal to that state. This precious jewel is in the Dhamma. By this truth may there be peace! (225)

5 The supreme Buddha praised pure meditation which gives instantaneous results. There is nothing equal to that meditation; This precious jewel is in the Dhamma. By this truth may there be peace! (226)

6 Eight individuals are praised by good people.[2] They constitute the four pairs.[3] They are the disciples of the Buddha, worthy of offerings. Whatever is offered to them yields abundant fruit. This precious jewel is in the Sangha. By this truth may there be peace! (227)

7 Those who are freed from desires are well established in the teaching of Gotama with firm mind. They have attained to that which should be attained, having plunged into immortal Nibbāna. They enjoy the Peace obtained without price. This precious jewel is in the Sangha. By this truth may there be peace! (228)

8 Just as a city gate fixed in the earth is not shaken by the winds from the four directions, even so, do I declare to be a good man he who thoroughly perceives the noble truths. This precious jewel is in the Sangha. By this truth may there be peace! (229)

9 Those who comprehend clearly the noble truths well taught by him who is endowed with profound wisdom, however exceedingly heedless they may be, they do not take birth for the eighth time. This precious jewel is in the Sangha. By this truth may there be peace! (230)

10 Three conditions are forsaken by him at the instant of acquisition of Insight,[4] namely, (i) self-delusion, (ii) doubt, and (iii) the indulgence in rites and ceremonies should there be any. He is also absolutely freed from the four states of misery[5] and is incapable of committing the six crimes.[6] This precious jewel is in the Sangha. By this truth may there be peace! (231)

11 Whatever evil deed he commits, either by his body, speech or thought, he is incapable of concealing it. For it has been said that such an act is impossible for one who has seen the Path.[7] This precious jewel is in the Sangha. By this truth may there be peace! (232)

12 As a clump of trees whose tops are blossoming during the first heat of the summer months, so the sublime doctrine leading to Nibbāna was taught for the highest goal. This precious jewel is in the Sangha. By this truth may there be peace! (233)

13 The excellent one, the knower of the excellent, the giver of the excellent and bringer of excellence has expounded the excellent doctrine. This precious jewel is in the Buddha. By this truth may there be peace! (234)

14 With the old (*kamma*) extinct, nothing new (*kamma*) to be reproduced, the mind detached from future birth — they have destroyed the seeds of existence. Their desires do not spring up again and those wise ones go out even as this lamp.[8] This precious jewel is in the Sangha. By this truth may there be peace! (235)

15 Whatever beings are assembled here, whether terrestrial or celestial, let us salute the Buddha. The Tathāgata is honoured by gods and men! May there be peace! (236)

16 Whatever beings are assembled here, whether terrestrial or celestial, let us salute the Dhamma. The Tathāgata is honoured by gods and men! May there be peace! (237)

17 Whatever beings are assembled here, whether terrestrial or celestial, let us salute the Sangha. The Tathāgata is honoured by gods and men! May there be peace! (238)

Notes

1 Jewel or gem. See Paramatthajotikā I, p. 165, II, p. 278, ed. Helmer Smith, Pali Text Society, London, repr. 1966.

2 Paramatthajotikā I, p. 275: *satam pasatthā ti sappurisehi Buddha-paccekabuddhasāvakehi aññehi ca devamanussehi pasatthā.*

3 Those who attain the first path, i.e., the stream-winner (*sotāpatti*) and its fruition and thus two become a pair; likewise the second, i.e. the once returner (*sakadāgāmi*), the third, i.e., non-returner (*anāgāmi*) and the worthy one (*arahatta*). Thus are formed the 'eight individuals'.

4 Insight (*dassana*): Path and Fruition of Stream-winning (*sotāpatti*).

5 (i) *Naraka* (state of woe), (ii) animal kingdom, (iii) ghost plane, (iv) demon world.

6 (i) Matricide, (ii) patricide, (iii) killing a saint, (iv) causing schisms in the Sangha, (v) wounding a Buddha, (vi) upholding wrong views.

7 Path (*pāda*) denotes the Stream-winning (*sotāpatti*), the stage at which the aspirant perceives Nibbāna for the first time.

8 Here Nibbāna has been illustrated with a simile of a lamp. Aśvaghoṣa versifies the same as follows: 'Just as a lamp, when it goes out neither hither nor thither, neither to the earth nor to the sky, neither in this direction nor to that, having been utterly blown out on account of the oil being consumed, similarly a sage obtains Nirvāṇa when the desires and passions have been consumed: he goes neither this way nor that, but obtains utter peace.' (*Saundaranandakāvya*, Ch. XVI, v. 28).

2. ĀMAGANDHA SUTTA

Stench

The spiritual meaning of 'impurity'

The ascetic Tissa addressed the Buddha Kassapa:

1 Millet, cingula beans and peas, edible leaves and roots, the fruit of any creeper; the virtuous who eat these, obtained justly, do not tell lies out of sensuous delight. (239)

2 O Kassapa, you who eat any food given by others, which is well-prepared, nicely arranged, pure and appealing; he who enjoys such food made with rice, eats [rotting flesh that emits a] stench. (240)

3 O brahmin, although you say that the charge of stench does not apply to you whilst eating rice with well-prepared fowl, yet I inquire the meaning of this from you: of what kind is your stench? (241)

4 The Buddha Kassapa: Taking life, beating, wounding, binding, stealing, lying, deceiving, worthless knowledge, adultery; this is stench. Not the eating of meat. (242)

5 In this world those individuals who are unrestrained in sensual pleasures, who are greedy for sweet things, who are associated with impure actions, who are of nihilistic views, crooked, difficult to follow; this is stench . . .[1] (243)

6 In this world those who are rude, arrogant, backbiting, treacherous, unkind, excessively egoistic, miserly, and do not give anything to anybody; this is stench . . . (244)

7 Anger, pride, obstinacy, antagonism, deceit, envy, boasting, excessive egoism, association with the immoral; this is stench . . . (245)

8 Those who are of bad morals, refuse to pay their debts, slanderous, deceitful in their dealings, pretentious, those who in this world, being the vilest of men, commit such wrong things; this is stench . . . (246)

9 Those persons who, in this world, are uncontrolled towards living beings, who are bent on injuring others, having taken their belongings; immoral, cruel, harsh, disrespectful; this is stench . . . (247)

10 Those who attack these living beings either out of greed or of hostility and are always bent upon evil, go to darkness after death, and fall headlong into woeful states; this is stench . . . (248)

11 Abstaining from fish and meat, nakedness, shaving of the head, matted hair, smearing with ashes, wearing rough deer-skins, attending the sacrificial fire; none of the various penances in the world performed for unhealthy ends, neither incantations, oblations, sacrifices nor seasonal observances, purify a person who has not overcome his doubts. (249)

12 He who lives with his senses guarded and conquered and is established in the Dhamma, delights in uprightness and gentleness; who has gone beyond attachments and has overcome all sorrows; that wise man does not cling to what is seen and heard. (250)

13 Thus the Buddha Kassapa preached this again and again. That ascetic who was well-versed in the [Vedic] hymns understood it. The sage who is free from defilements, non-attached and difficult to follow, uttered this [discourse] in beautiful stanzas. (251)

14 Thus, having listened to the well-spoken words of the Buddha who is free from defilements, which end all misery, he worshipped the Tathāgata with humble mind and requested to be admitted into the Order at that very place. (252)

Note

1 From 5 to 10 each stanza ends with the refrain, 'Not the eating of meat.'

3. HIRI[1] SUTTA

Shame

On true friendship

The Buddha delivered this discourse to a brahmin of Sāvatthi who wished to know the answers to the following four questions:

i With whom should one not associate?
ii With whom should one associate?
iii What brings happiness?
iv What is the sweetest condition?

1 Know this well that 'He is not my friend' who behaves shamelessly and who despises his friend, while saying 'I am your friend' without undertaking any work he can do for him. (253)

2 The wise know him as a mere talker, but not a doer.[2] One who uses pleasant words to friends, but does not act accordingly. (254)

3 He is not a friend who is always anxiously alert in a conflict, and who is only looking out for defects. He is, indeed, a friend who is incapable of being separated from you by others, like a son on his father's breast. (255)

4 One who bears human responsibility which yields good result, who cultivates that cause which gives joy and brings praise and happiness. (256)

5 Having drunk the sweetness of solitude and also the sweetness of tranquility, one becomes free from fear and wrongdoing while drinking the sweetness of the joy of truth.[3] (257)

Notes

1 *Hiri* means the sense of shame in committing any immoral act, i.e., the shame which deters a person from doing what is wrong.

2 *Ananvayan ti yaṃ atthaṃ dassāmi karissāmī ti bhāsati tena ananugataṃ*. Sutta-Nipāta Commentary.
3 Cf. Dhammapada, v. 205.

4. MAHĀMAṄGALA SUTTA

The Auspicious Performance

The definition of the highest blessing

Thus have I heard: Once the Buddha was living near Sāvatthi in the Jeta Grove at Anāthapiṇḍika's monastery. Then, one beautiful night, a certain devatā, having illumined the whole Jeta Grove with surpassing splendour, came to the Buddha and, making salutations, stood on one side and addressed the Buddha in [the following] verse:

1 Many gods and men, wishing for well-being, have pondered over those things that constitute auspicious performances. Tell us what is the highest auspicious performance.[1] (258)

The Buddha:

2 Not to associate with fools, but to associate with the wise and to honour those who are worthy of honour; this is the most auspicious performance. (259)

3 To reside in a congenial environment, to have done meritorious deeds in the past and to set oneself in the right course; this is the most auspicious performance. (260)

4 A good, all-round, education, [appreciation of] the Arts, a highly-trained discipline and pleasant speech; this is the most auspicious performance. (261)

5 Supporting one's father and mother, cherishing wife and children and a peaceful occupation; this is the most auspicious performance. (262)

6 Liberality, dutiful conduct, the helping of relatives and blameless actions; this is the most auspicious performance. (263)

7 Ceasing and abstaining from evil, abstention from intoxicating drinks and diligence in virtue; this is the most auspicious performance. (264)

8 Reverence, humility, contentment, gratitude and timely hearing of the Dhamma; this is the most auspicious performance. (265)

9 Forbearance, obedience, association with exemplars of the Dhamma-life and participation in religious discussions; this is the most auspicious performance. (266)

10 Self-control, perception of the Noble Truths and the realization of Nibbāna; this is the most auspicious performance. (267)

11 If one's mind is sorrowless, stainless and secure [in Nibbāna] and is not disturbed when affected by worldly vicissitudes;[2] this is the most auspicious performance. (268)

12 Those who thus acting are everywhere unconquered, attain happiness everywhere — to them these are the most auspicious performances. (269)

Notes

1 Highest performance, great happiness or blessing.

2 Primarily the following pairs of worldly vicissitudes or conditions are connected with one's life: gain and loss, success and defeat, praise and blame, happiness and sorrow.

5. SŪCILOMA SUTTA

Sūciloma

A discourse similar to the Āḷavaka Sutta (above)

Thus have I heard: Once when the Buddha was spending some time at Gayā on a stone couch in the abode of the yakkha Sūciloma, the yakkhas Khara and Sūciloma were passing nearby [and the former asked] 'Is this man an ascetic?' Sūciloma replied: 'He's no ascetic but merely feigning his appearance. However, I'll make sure.' Then Sūciloma went up to the Buddha and tried to press himself against his body but the Buddha drew back from his touch. Thereupon Sūciloma asked the Buddha: 'O ascetic, are you afraid of me?' The Buddha replied: 'Friend, I am not afraid of you, but your touch is unpleasant.'

Sūciloma: I shall ask you a question, O ascetic; if you fail to answer it I'll drive you out of your wits, or tear out your heart, or take you by your feet and fling you to the other side of the Ganges.

The Buddha: I do not see, friend, in the world a person who could do so. However, friend, ask any question you like.

1 Sūciloma: From where do passion and hate spring? From where do discontentment, attachment and terror spring? From where do evil speculations arise and harass the mind as do boys a crow? (270)

2 The Buddha: Passion and hatred spring from egoism. So do discontentment, attachment and terror. Speculative thoughts also spring therefrom and harass the mind as do boys a crow. (271)

3 They spring from desire, are in one's self like the shoots which spring from the branches of a banyan tree. They are attached to sense desires like a māluvā creeper which overgrows the jungle. (272)

4 Listen, O yakkha, those who know the source, overcome it. They cross the flood which is difficult to cross and which has never been crossed before, and are no more reborn. (273)

6. DHAMMĀCARIYA SUTTA

The Good Life

The monks are recommended to expel those liable to detract from their leading a pure life

1 If one renounces household life, becomes a recluse and leads a pure and celibate life; this is the worthiest[1] jewel. (274)

2 However, if he be, by nature, garrulous, and brutishly derives pleasure from injuring others, the life of such a one becomes unprofitable and his defilements increase. (275)

3 A monk who delights in quarrelling, being veiled by delusion, does not understand the doctrine preached by the Buddha even when explained. (276)

4 Led by ignorance, he does not understand that injuring those whose minds are well composed, is misconduct that leads to a woeful state. (277)

5 That kind of monk, certainly, will experience misery after death, going to places of suffering from birth to birth, from darkness to [greater] darkness. (278)

6 Like a cess-pool filled over a number of years, such an impure one is difficult to be purified. (279)

7 O monks, if you should know such a one who is attached to the worldly life, having unwholesome desires, ulterior motives, and of evil modes of behaviour. (280)

8 Ostracise and oust him, all being united; as dust, sweep him out, as refuse, remove him. (281)

9 Then remove those hollow ones who, not being monks, yet pretend to be so; eject those possessing the aforementioned undesirable traits of character. (282)

10 Be pure and associate with the pure; being mindful, united and arise; put an end to suffering. (283)

Note

1 I think *vasu* means wealth. The commentary also says *vasuttaman ti uttamaratanaṃ*.

7. BRĀHMAṆADHAMMIKA SUTTA

The Good Conduct of the Brahmin

The Buddha describes the ideal mode of life of brahmins in the 'Golden Age' and how they degenerated

Thus have I heard: Once the Buddha was living near Sāvatthi in the Jeta Grove at Anāthapiṇḍika's monastery. Then a great many wealthy brahmins of Kosala, decrepit, elderly, old, advanced in years, arrived at old age, went to where the Buddha was residing and were highly pleased with seeing him. Having exchanged friendly speech causing delight and worthy of being remembered, They sat down on one side and asked the Buddha: 'Venerable Gotama, are the brahmins of the present day found engaged in the priestly duties of the ancient brahmins?'

'The brahmins of the present day are not, indeed, found engaged in the priestly duties of the ancient brahmins'.

'It will be good of you, Gotama, if you will explain them, if it is not inconvenient to you.'

The Buddha:

1 The sages of ancient times, possessed of self-control and restrained mind, abandoning the fivefold sensual pleasures, led a life for their own welfare. (284)

2 The brahmins of ancient times had no cattle, neither gold nor corn. Learning was wealth and corn for them; they protected this divine treasure. (285)

3 Whatever food prepared for them was placed at the door — they considered that it was prepared through devotion to those seekers. (286)

4 Prosperous people from the provinces and outside countries worshipped those brahmins with garments of various colours, beds and dwellings. (287)

5 The brahmins were neither injured nor conquered. They were protected by virtue. No one ever opposed them at the entrance of any household. (288)

6 Formerly the brahmins practised celibacy from their youth up to their forty-eighth year. They were engaged in search of learning and good conduct. (289)

7 The brahmins cohabited not with another's wife nor did they buy a wife. Being brought by mutual love to love together, they were pleased with each other. (290)

8 The brahmins cohabited not except with a wife whose menstrual discharge had ceased and at no other time but the right time. (291)

9 They praised chastity, morality, integrity, amiability, penance, gentleness, non-violence and forbearance. (292)

10 If there was any brahmin of great influence, who was the noblest of them, even he was chaste and did not even in dreams indulge in sexual intercourse. (293)

11 Here, some wise men, following his precepts, praised chastity, morality and forbearance. (294)

12 Having begged for rice, beds, cloth, butter, oil and collecting them by fair means, they offered such objects as these for sacrifice, and at the sacrifice they did not kill cows. (295)

13 The cows by means of which medicinal drugs are produced are our great friends, like our mother, father, brother and other relations. (296)

14 They give food, strength, beauty, health — knowing these benefits, they did not kill cattle. (297)

15 The brahmins were graceful, large-bodied, handsome and honoured, very attentive to their duties and zealous as to what should be done and what should not be done. This community thus prospered happily in the world as long as they lived accordingly. (298)

16 Having seen worthless things such as wealth and well-adorned women, however, there was a change in them. (299)

17 – 18 The brahmins coveted the great enjoyments of men surrounded by herds of cows, groups of beautiful women, chariots with well-trained horses, well decorated with beautiful curtains and homes and dwelling places built to good proportion. (300 – 1)

19 Composing hymns, they then approached the king, Okkāka, and said: 'You are possessed of manifold wealth; offer us your vast riches; offer us your immense wealth.' (302)

20 Then the king, the lord of chariots, persuaded by the brahmins, performed freely the horse sacrifice, the human sacrifice, the water rites and the sacrifice of liquor. Having performed these sacrifices, he gave wealth to the brahmins. (303)

21 Cattle, beds, garments, adorned women, well-made chariots drawn by noble horses and covers of various embroidery. (304)

22 Beautiful houses, well planned into apartments, filling these with various kinds of grain — thus gave this wealth to the brahmins. (305)

23 And they having thus received wealth desired to hoard; and being overwhelmed by covetousness their greed increased. They composed hymns and again approached Okkāka. (306)

24 'Like water, earth, gold and corn — even so are the cattle, for they are the necessary appendage of living beings. Therefore, offer us your immense wealth, give us your vast riches.' (307)

25 Then the king, the lord of chariots, persuaded by the brahmins caused to be killed many hundred thousand cattle in sacrifice. (308)

26 Neither with their legs nor with their horns do the cows hurt anybody, being obedient like lambs and yielding jars of milk. The king, seizing them by the horns, had them killed by a sword. (309)

27 Then the gods, the ancestors, Indra, the titans and the demons cried out as the sword fell on the cows: 'This is unjust!' (310)

28 In ancient days there were only three diseases: desire, hunger and decay; but owing to the killing of animals, these sprang to ninety-eight. (311)

29 This old injustice has come down. The innocent cows are killed. The sacrificing priests have fallen from virtue. (312)

30 Thus this ancient, mean practice is censured by the wise. Wherever such a practice is seen people blame the sacrificing priest. (313)

31 Thus, dutiful conduct being destroyed, the workmen and traders were divided, the warriors were also widely separated. The wife disregarded her husband. (314)

32 The warriors, brahmins and others who protected their castes, disregarding their caste, came under the influence of sensual pleasure. (315)

It being thus spoken, the brahmins of great wealth said thus to the Buddha: 'It is amazing, Venerable Gotama, it is wonderful, Venerable Gotama! Just as if one might raise what has been overturned, or reveal what has been hidden, or point out the way to him who has gone astray, or hold out a lamp in the dark so that those who have eyes may see objects, so likewise has the Truth been explained by Venerable Gotama in various ways. Therefore, we take refuge in him, his Dhamma and his Sangha. May the Venerable Gotama accept us as lay followers who henceforth have taken refuge in him for the rest of our lives.'

8. NĀVĀ[1] SUTTA

The Boat

On choosing a good and learned teacher

1 That man should venerate him from whom he learns the Dhamma as the gods venerate Indra. The learned person thus being venerated, being pleased with the disciple, makes the Dhamma manifest. (316)

2 Having paid attention to it and considered it, the wise man, putting the Dhamma into practice, becomes learned, intelligent and accomplished and, being vigilant, he associates with such a teacher. (317)

3 One who follows an inferior and foolish teacher who has not realized the meaning, and who is jealous, approaches death without comprehending the Dhamma and unrelieved of doubt. (318)

4 As a man who has fallen into an overflowing river with deep water and a rapid current; carried away by a swift-flowing current, how can he help others to cross it? (319)

5 Even so, he who has not comprehended the Dhamma, has not paid attention to its meaning as expounded by the learned, being himself without knowledge — how can he make others understand? (320)

6 As one who, having boarded a boat firmly equipped with oars and a rudder, and knowing the method, is skilful and wise, by means of it he causes many others to cross over. (321)

7 Even so, he who has attained knowledge and has a well-trained mind, who is learned and unmoved; clearly knows he can help others to understand, who are attentive to listen and ready to comprehend. (322)

8 Therefore, one should surely associate with a good man who is wise and learned. He should know the meaning and practise accordingly and, gaining understanding of the Dhamma, will attain happiness. (323)

Note

1 Boat or ship; Sutta-Nipāta Commentary: Dhamma, thus it is also called *Dhamma Sutta*.

9. KIṂSĪLA SUTTA

Right Conduct

Sāriputta:
1 A man of what character, of what conduct, by performing what actions, will be well established and will attain the highest well-being? (324)

The Buddha:
2 Let him be one who honours his elders; who is not envious, knows the right time for seeing the teacher, knows the right moment to listen attentively to the discourses well preached by him. (325)

3 Let him go to the presence of his teachers at the right time; be obedient, discarding obstinacy. Let him remember and practise the teaching, self-restraint and virtue. (326)

4 One who rejoices and delights in the Dhamma and who is well-established in it; one who does not speak in opposition to the Dhamma; one who refrains from unprofitable conversation, let him pass his time with true and well-spoken words. (327)

5 Having abandoned laughter, gossip, complaining, ill-will, deception, hypocrisy, greediness, spite, bad temper, impurity and attachment, let him live free from pride, with steady mind. (328)

6 The essence of well-spoken words is understanding. The essence of learning and understanding is concentration. The wisdom and learning of the man who is hasty and negligent do not increase. (329)

7 Those who delight in the teaching taught by the Noble Ones are unique in speech, mind and action; are established in peace, gentleness and meditation, and obtain the essence of learning and wisdom. (330)

10. UṬṬHĀNA SUTTA

Arousing

An urgent exhortation to exert effort

Arise! sit up!
What advantage is there in your sleeping;
What sleep is there to those who are afflicted by disease,
Pierced by the arrow of suffering? (331)

Arise! Sit up!
Train yourselves resolutely to attain Peace.
Do not let the King of Evil [Māra] knowing you are negligent,
Delude you and place you under his control. (332)

Overcome this craving
To which gods and men remain attached and seek pleasure.
Do not let the opportune moment[1] pass.
Those who let the opportune moment pass
Grieve when they are consigned to woe. (333)

Negligence is a taint
And so is the taint which falls
Continuously, from negligence to negligence,
By earnestness and knowledge
Let one pluck out his dart [of passions]. (334)

Note

1 Opportunity or moment is called *khaṇa* and *akkhaṇa* means inopportune moments. According to the Saṅgiti Sutta of the Dīgha Nikāya, there are 9

inopportune moments for a human being who is unable to follow the teaching of a Buddha: At the time of the appearance of a Buddha one is reborn in (1) the state of woe (*niraya*), (2) the animal kingdom, (3) among spirits, (4) Titans, (5) in some long-lived *deva* community, (6) among unintelligent barbarians (7) or those who hold wrong views, (8) or reborn as stupid, dull, deaf or dumb (9) or at a time when a Buddha is not born. The Saddhammopāyana, ed. R. Morris, *Journal of the Pali Text Society*, VI, London 1887 (repr. 1978), enumerates only 8 inopportune moments (see vv. 4–6). A work of the (Sinhalese) Abhayagirivāsins, this text excludes (4). See the Upāsakajanālaṇkāra, ed. H. Saddhatissa, Pali Text Society, London 1965, p. 61.

11. RĀHULA SUTTA

Rāhula

The Buddha recommends the life of a recluse to his son, Rāhula

The Buddha:

1 Do you not despise the wise man by constantly living with him? Is the holder of the torch to mankind honoured by you? (335)

Rāhula:

2 I do not despise the wise man by constantly living with him. The holder of the torch to mankind is always honoured by me. (336)

The Buddha:

3 Discarding the five pleasures of sense, enticing and delightful to the mind, renouncing the home through confidence, be one who puts an end to suffering. (337)

4 Associate with good friends; resort to a remote dwelling place, which is secluded and quiet. Be moderate in eating. (338)

5 Do not crave for these things; robes, food, medicines and dwelling. Do not be one who returns to the world. (339)

6 Have restraint according to the disciplinary code. Be restrained in the five senses. Be mindful of the body and continually develop dispassion. (340)

7 Avoid lustful signs which are connected with passion. Cultivate your mind which is concentrated and undisturbed on the impurities of the body. (341)

8 Meditate on the Signless [Nibbāna]. Forsake the tendency of egoism. Thereby ending such egoism you will live calmly. (342)

Thus the Buddha constantly advised Venerable Rāhula by these stanzas.

12. VAṄGĪSA SUTTA[1]

Vaṅgīsa

Vaṅgīsa receives confirmation that his teacher has attained Nibbāna

Once the Buddha resided near Āḷavi at a shrine called Aggāḷava. At that time the Venerable Nigrodhakappa, the preceptor of Venerable Vaṅgīsa, had passed away there not long before. Then a thought occurred to the Venerable Vaṅgīsa (who lived in solitude) during his private meditations as to whether his preceptor had attained Nibbāna or not. Then, rising from his retirement in the evening, Venerable Vaṅgīsa [accompanied by his colleagues] approached the Buddha and with due respect he questioned thus:

1 We ask the Buddha of great wisdom, the remover of doubts in this world — the well-known monk, possessor of glory and peaceful mind, who died at Aggāḷava. (343)

2 O Buddha, the name Nigrodhakappa was given to him by you. Being strenuous, he wandered about venerating you, aspiring to liberation, firm in the perception of the Dhamma. (344)

3 O Buddha, the All-seeing One, we all wish to know about that disciple. We are ready to hear, you are our Master, you are incomparable. (345)

4 Cut off our doubt, tell us about this. O you of extensive wisdom, make known to us whether he has attained Nibbāna. O you, All-seeing One, speak in the midst of us as the thousand-eyed Indra, the king of gods. (346)

5 Whatever knots there are in the world, leading to delusion, associated with ignorance, causing doubt, all these are untied when one comes to the Tathāgata: indeed his eye is the greatest for all men. (347)

6 If a man such as you, did not dispel passions as wind dispels the clouds, the whole world would be covered with darkness; not even illustrious men would shine. (348)

7 Wise men are the enlighteners. For certain I think you are a wise one. We have come to you, endowed with insight and knowledge. Will you reveal the position of Venerable Nigrodhakappa to us in the midst of this assembly? (349)

8 O lovely one, quickly raise your sweet voice as a swan stretching forth its neck with a rich and well-regulated voice. We will all listen to you attentively. (350)

9 We earnestly request you, the pure one who has overcome birth and death completely, to proclaim the Dhamma, for this is not a mere fulfilment of the desire of those who are worldlings. Let the Tathāgata act with wisdom. (351)

10 The explanations from you who are endowed with guileless wisdom have always been accepted. This final folding of hands is well raised. O supreme sage, do not keep us in ignorance. (352)

11 Knowing thoroughly the teaching of the noble ones, O you who are of untiring energy, do not leave us in ignorance. As one suffering from heat in the hot season longs for water, we long for your words, so please shower your words of wisdom. (353)

12 If Venerable Nigrodhakappa led a holy life, was this fruitful? Did he attain Nibbāna with residue left behind? How was he liberated, that we long to hear. (354)

13 The Buddha: He cut off the desire for mind and matter in this world which was Māra's stream flowing for a long time; he has crossed completely all births and deaths. Thus said the Blessed One, the chief of the first five disciplines.[2] (355)

14 You are the noblest of the great sages. Hearing your words I am pleased. My inquiry has not been in vain. The Buddha did not delude me. (356)

15 The Buddha's disciple was one who acted as you said. He has cut asunder the outspread and strong net of deceitful Māra. (357)

16 O Blessed One, the Venerable Nigrodhakappa saw the source of grasping and certainly crossed the realm of death so difficult to cross. (358)

Notes

1 Also called the *Nigrodhakappa Sutta*.

2 *Pañcaseṭṭho*: in another sense, this implies that the Buddha overpowered the five senses.

13. SAMMĀPARIBBĀJANIYA SUTTA

The Correct Homeless Life

Questioner:

1 I ask the sage of great wisdom who has crossed [the flood of existence] and gone over to the other shore, who has attained Nibbāna and is steadfast: How should a monk properly lead a homeless life after going forth from the household life and having repelled the sense desires? (359)

The Buddha:

2 In him whom belief in the efficacy of omens like shooting stars, dreams and signs is destroyed; that monk who has avoided the resulting consquences would properly lead a homeless life. (360)

3 Let the monk give up the desire for sense pleasure, either earthly or heavenly and passing beyond existence and understanding the Teaching, he would . . .[1] (361)

4 Let the monk refrain from slander and give up anger and greed and be free from attraction and repulsion. He would . . . (362)

5 Having given up what is pleasant and unpleasant, grasping at nothing, not dependent upon anything, being free from the fetters, he would . . . (363)

6 Not seeing any value in material belongings, removing strong desire for grasping objects, being one who is unattached and who is not led by others, he would . . . (364)

7 Being one who is not opposed to anyone, either by word, thought or deed, understanding the Teaching well, aspiring to the state of Nibbāna, he would . . . (365)

8 The monk who did not become elated, thinking, 'the people respect me', and when abused did not feel ill-will; and receiving food from others did not become exhilarated, he would . . . (366)

9 The monk who, abandoning craving and becoming, abstaining from harming and obstructing others, has overcome doubt and removed the arrow [of desire], he would . . . (367)

10 The monk who, knowing what is suitable for himself, would not hurt anyone in the world; realizing the Teaching as it really is, he would . . . (368)

11 He in whom there are no latent evil tendencies whatsoever and all the roots of evil have been destroyed; who, overcoming desires, has freed himself from them, he would . . . (369)

12 One whose depravities are destroyed, who has abandoned egoism, who has completely escaped from the path of passion, who is restrained, emancipated and steadfast, he would . . . (370)

13 One who is confident, learned, who sees the path leading to Nibbāna, a wise man who does not take sides with quarrelling sects; who has removed greed, anger and ill-will, he would . . . (371)

14 He who has conquered the defilements, who has torn asunder the veil of evil, who is well disciplined in the Teaching, who has gone to the other shore [Nibbāna], who is firm and skilful in the knowledge concerning the destruction of *kamma*-producing tendencies, he would . . . (372)

15 One who has transcended egoistic thought in relation to the past and future, who is of exceedingly clear wisdom, who is released from all sensual objects, he would . . . (373)

16 Having realized the Truth, having understood the Teaching, having seen clearly the destruction of the depravities, by the elimination of all attachments, he would . . . (374)

Questioner:

17 Certainly, Blessed One, it is so: the monk who lives thus, restrained and having overcome all fetters, would properly lead a homeless life. (375)

Note

1 From 3 to 16 each stanza ends with the refrain, 'he would properly lead a homeless life.'

14. DHAMMIKA SUTTA

Dhammika

Synopses of the monk and lay lives

Thus have I heard: Once when the Buddha was dwelling near Sāvatthi in the Jeta Grove at Anāthapiṇḍika's monastery, the lay disciple, Dhammika, accompanied by five hundred colleagues, visited him. After paying their respects they took their seats and Dhammika addressed the Buddha:

1 O Gotama of great wisdom, I ask you: Acting in what manner does a disciple who goes from home to a homeless life, or one who is still a good lay devotee, act well? (376)

2 For you know the course of the world including that of the gods and also the way beyond [Nibbāna]. There are none comparable with you who see the subtle meanings of things. They say that you are, indeed, the most excellent and Englightened One. (377)

3 Realizing all wisdom and being merciful to all sentient beings you expounded the Dhamma. You are the destroyer of the veil of ignorance. You are the possessor of eyes on every aspect. Stainless, you illumine the whole world. (378)

4 The king of elephants, Erāvaṇa, hearing you were the Conqueror, came near to you. After listening, he made an utterance of delight and went away, saying 'Excellent'. (379)

5 The king, Vessavaṇa Kuvera, called upon you to [ask a] question on the Dhamma. When you were so questioned by him, O Wise One, you spoke to him and he, also, after listening, was delighted. (380)

6 None of those disputing heretics, whether fallacious reasoners (Ājīvikas) or bondless ascetics (Nigaṇṭhas) can overcome you by wisdom, as one who is stationary cannot overtake the one who walks swiftly. (381)

7 Those disputing brahmins, whosoever they may be, who are experienced, and others considered to be disputants, all of them expect some explanation from you. (382)

8 Indeed, this Dhamma, subtle and pleasant, which has been well preached by you, O Blessed One, we all are longing to hear. O noble Buddha, will you speak to us when you are requested? (383)

9 Let all these monks as well as lay disciples sitting down together hear the Dhamma realized by the Stainless One, as gods hear the well-spoken words of Indra. (384)

The Buddha:
10 O monks, listen to me, I shall make you hear the pure Dhamma. Will you bear it in mind! Let the wise man who is intent upon his own progress practise the way of deportment suitable for a renounced one. (385)

11 The monk should not be wandering at the wrong time but should go to the village for alms at the right time. Temptations cling to him who wanders at an improper time. Therefore, the wise ones do not wander at the wrong time. (386)

12 Forms, sounds, tastes, odours and contacts completely intoxicate people; putting away the desire for these things he should go at the right time for the morning meal. (387)

13 The monk having thus obtained his meal and returned alone, should sit in solitude; reflecting within himself, he should be self-composed, avoiding distractions. (388)

14 If he speaks with a follower or with anybody else or with a fellow-monk, he should speak of the excellent Dhamma. He should not slander nor speak ill of others. (389)

15 Some put forward controversial arguments. We do not praise the people of lower understanding. Temptations from here and there ensnare them, for their minds become deeply involved in them. (390)

16 The follower of the noblest Wise One, on hearing the doctrine taught by him, should make use of food, lodging, bed, seat, water, and clean his robe with due care. (391)

17 Therefore, in being detached from these things, the monk must be as a drop of water on a lotus leaf. (392)

18 Now I will tell you of the rules of conduct for a householder, acting according to which, he becomes a good disciple. If there be monk-duty to be performed, such duty cannot be fulfilled by him who possesses household property. (393)

19 Let him not destroy life nor cause others to destroy life and, also, not approve of others' killing. Let him refrain from oppressing all living beings in the world, whether strong or weak. (394)

20 Then because the disciple knows that it belongs to others, stealing anything from any place should be avoided. Let him not cause to steal, nor approve of others' stealing. All stealing should be avoided. (395)

21 The wise man should avoid non-celibate life as if it were a burning charcoal pit. If he is unable to lead a celibate life fully, let him not transgress with another's wife. (396)

22 Whether he is in an assembly or in a public place let him not tell lies to another. Let him not cause others to tell lies nor approve of others' telling lies. (397)

23 The householder who delights in self-control, knowing that taking intoxicants results in its loss, should not indulge in taking intoxicants nor should he cause others to take them nor approve of others' doing so. (398)

24 Fools commit evil deeds as a result of drunkenness and cause other people, who are negligent, to act accordingly. One should avoid this sphere of evil deeds, this madness, this delusion, this delight of fools. (399)

25 (i) One should not destroy life; (ii) should not take that which is not given; (iii) should not tell lies; (iv) should not be a drinker; (v) should refrain from all unchastity; (vi) should not eat untimely food at night. (400)

26 (vii) One should not wear ornaments nor use perfumes; (viii) should lie on a mat spread on the ground. This they call an eightfold sacred observance proclaimed by the Buddha who came to do away with sorrow. (401)

27 Being happy-minded one should observe this virtue of eight precepts on the fourteenth, fifteenth and eighth days of the lunar fortnight [and during the *Pāṭihāriyapakkha* — the three rainy months together with those preceding and following this season, five months in all]. (402)

28 Then on the following morning, the wise one who has observed eight precepts should happily provide the Community of Monks with food and drink in a suitable manner. (403)

29 Let him support his father and mother in a proper manner and also pursue a blameless career. The householder observing these duties with diligence is reborn in the sphere of 'self-luminant' beings. (404)

III. The Great Chapter

1. PABBAJJĀ SUTTA

The Going Forth

of the Buddha and his encounter with King Bimbisāra

1 I shall tell you about the renunciation, the manner in which the one with insight renounced the world and the manner of his inquiry which led him to choose the life of renunciation. (405)

2 'In a home', thought that man, 'a life is stifled — impurity is everywhere like dust.' 'For the wanderer', thought that man, 'there is space — he lives out in the open, in the air.' He saw this was so and set off. (406)

3 He was now a wanderer. So he worked to purify his life: in everything he did and in everything he said he avoided the unwholesome and the bad. (407)

4 And as he, the Buddha, the one full of noble characteristics, walked about in search of food he came in time to Rājagaha, in Magadha. (408)

5 The king, Bimbisāra, stood in his palace and, seeing the one possessing the noble characteristics, called out to his followers: (409)

6–7 'Look carefully, friends, he is handsome, shapely and of beautiful complexion. His gait is pleasing with his eyes cast at only a little distance; with downcast eyes he is mindful and he does not seem to be from a low family. Send out the palace messengers to find out where he's going.' (410–11)

8 So the king's men were sent out and they followed him inquiring, 'Where is the monk going? Where is he planning to stay?' (412)

9 The beggar walked on from house to house watching the sense doors, well restrained, alert and mindful. Soon his bowl was full. (413)

10 When his begging-round was over he set off [for the hills] and made his way towards mount Paṇḍava. The messengers now knew that he would stay there. (414)

11 Seeing that he was going to stay there, some sat down and watched while another messenger went back to inform the king. (415)

12 'Your Majesty', he said, 'the monk has settled down on the east side of mount Paṇḍava. He's sitting there in his mountain lair like a lion or a tiger or a bull!' (416)

13 Hearing the messenger's words the warrior king had his special chariot prepared and then set off with the greatest haste to mount Paṇḍava. (417)

14 The king went as far as he could go by the chariot and then got off and walked up the mountain to the monk. (418)

15 He sat down beside him, exchanged greetings and respects, and then spoke thus: (419)

16 'You are only a young man, sir, a lad in the prime of your life. You are handsome and shapely. You appear to be a prince of noble birth. (420)

17 Adorning a splendid army, esteemed by a council of nobles, enjoy wealth which I can bestow upon you. However, can you please tell me what family you're from?' (421)

18 'King', came the answer, 'not far from Himavant, the snowland, is a country called Kosala. The people of Kosala are rich and they are strong. (422)

19 They come from the race of the sun and their family name is Sākya. That was the people I left when I walked away from the wish and the longing for pleasure. (423)

20 I have seen the miseries of pleasure. I have seen the security involved in renouncing them;

So now I will go,
I will go on into the struggle,
This is to my mind delight;
This is where my mind finds bliss.' (424)

2. PADHĀNA SUTTA

The Striving

of the Buddha against temptation

1 I was living on the bank of the Nerañjara river engaged in deep struggle, practising meditation with all my strength in the effort to find freedom from bondage. (425)

2 Māra came up to me and started talking to me in words appearing to be full of sympathy: 'You're so thin and pale', he said, 'Why — you're near to death! (426)

3 I'll bet a thousand to one you're going to die — there's only the slightest chance that you'll survive! My dear sir, do live! It's far better to live — you could accumulate merit if you stayed alive. (427)

4 You could lead the religious life, perform the offerings to the fire (god) — it's a sure way to get lots of merit. What's the point of all this exertion? (428)

5 The path of exertion and struggle is difficult, hard and strenuous, and full of troubles.' Uttering these verses, Māra stood right next to the Buddha. (429)

6 Then the Buddha told Māra who was uttering such words: 'Why have you come here, evil one, you friend of negligence? (430)

7 I do not need the least merit you speak of. O Māra, you should preach about merits to those who need them. (431)

8 I have confidence and energy and knowledge as well. So have I engaged myself in effort. Why do you inquire about my life? (432)

9 When the wind blows, even rivers and streams are dried up. So why shouldn't it dry up my blood while I am deep in struggle? (433)

10 As the blood dries up, so too will bile and phlegm. The body may be wasting away, but the mind gets more and more settled. More and more do mindfulness, wisdom and concentration get established in me. (434)

11 While living in this manner experiencing the extremes of sensation my mind no longer aspires for sensuous pleasures. (435)

12 The foremost of your armies is that of Desire, the second is called Dislike. The third is Hunger-Thirst and the fourth is Craving. (436)

13 The fifth is the army of Lethargy-Laziness and the sixth is Fear. The seventh is Doubt and the eighth is Obstinacy-Restlessness. (437)

14 Then there are also material gain, praise, honour and fame obtained by wrongful means. One may also think highly of oneself and disparage others. (438)

15 These, O Māra, are your forces, the attackers of the evil one. One less than a hero will not be victorious over them and attain happiness. (439)

16 Look: do you see this strand of muñja grass I am wearing? I do not care for life. I would rather die in this conflict than be alive but defeated. (440)

17 There are monks and hermits who have drowned [in defilements] and never see that path which the well-conducted ones tread. (441)

18 I can see the troops all around me, with Māra mounted on an elephant, and I go forward into the struggle. (442)

19 Even though the whole world, inclusive of its gods, cannot beat that army of yours, I am going to destroy it with the power of wisdom like an unfired clay pot with a stone. (443)

20 With disciplined thought and firmly grounded mindfulness I shall travel from country to country training numerous disciples. (444)

21 Alert and energetic in the practice of my teaching, contrary to your wish, they will attain that which having attained they will not come to grief.' (445)

22 'I've followed the Blessed One for seven years', said Māra, 'and I've watched every step he's made. And not once have I had access to him, who's completely enlightened and mindful. (446)

23 I remember once seeing a crow hovering above a lump of fat on the ground below. "Ah, food!" it thought. But the lump turned out to be a rock, hard and inedible, and the crow flew away disgusted. (447)

24 We've had enough; it's like that crow eating rock for us; we're going away, we're finished with Gotama!' (448)

25 Māra was so upset by his failure that he dropped the lute he was carrying, and at the moment it fell to the ground the evil-minded yakkha disappeared. (449)

3. SUBHĀSITA SUTTA

Good Words

Thus have I heard: Once, when the Buddha was staying in the Jeta Grove, near Sāvatthi, he said to his monks:

'Speech which has four characteristics is speech well spoken, blameless and not censured by the wise; namely, the speech of a monk who speaks only what is wholesome and not what is unwholesome, who speaks only what is worthy and not what is unworthy, who speaks only what is pleasant and not what is unpleasant, who speaks only what is truthful and not what is untruthful. Speech characterized by these four factors is well spoken, and not ill spoken, blameless and not censured by the wise.' That is what the Master said, and having said this he went on, as Teacher, to say this:

1 'Wholesome speech, the saints say is the foremost.
One should speak what is worthy and not what is unworthy and this is the second.
One should speak what is pleasant and not what is unpleasant and this is the third.
One should speak what is truthful and not what is false and this is the fourth.' (450)

Then a monk called Vangīsa got up from his seat and went up to the Buddha. He respectfully placed his robe over one shoulder and with his hands placed together asked the Master for permission to speak. Having obtained it, he spoke these appropriate words of praise:

2 'Let us use words that do not cause us pain.
Let us use words that do not hurt each other:
Those, truly, are wholesome words. (451)

3 Let us use pleasant speech, where the words make people glad,
Not resorting to evil speech, let us use pleasant speech on others. (452)

4 The words of truth are immortal. This is an eternal nature. As the old saying goes, words of truth cannot die. And good people, they say, are well grounded in truth, welfare and virtue. (453)

5 And the words which the Buddha speaks, words that lead to blowing out, putting an end to suffering, are the worthiest words.' (454)

4. PŪRAḶĀSA[1] SUTTA

The Sacrificial Cake

On whom to bestow offerings

Thus have I heard: Once the Buddha was staying in Kosala, on the bank of the River Sundarika. Nearby, a brahmin called Sundarika-Bhāradvāja was busy performing sacred rituals and burning offerings on a fire. When the brahmin had finished his rituals, he got up from his seat and looked around. 'Who shall I give the remains of my offerings to?' he asked. Then, not far away, he noticed the Buddha sitting under a tree, completely covered by his robe. So, with the offerings in one hand and the water jar in the other, the brahmin walked over to the Buddha. As he heard the brahmin's footsteps the Buddha uncovered his head. 'Why', thought the brahmin, 'this man's had his head shaved, he's nothing but a shaveling!', and he thought of turning back. But then he thought, 'Some of the brahmins have also shaved their heads. I had better go and ask him what family he's from.' So he went up to the Buddha and said, 'What caste are you?' And the Buddha made his answer to the brahmin:

1 'I am not a brahmin. Nor am I a prince, or a farmer, or anything else. I have come to understand clearly how worldly people are born; now I wander through the world as a wise man, without possessions, with nothing. (455)

2 I wear a double robe, I have shaved off my hair. And I wander, without a home, without the need to mix with people in this world; fully calmed. Your question about caste is irrelevant.' (456)

3 'But, Sir', said the brahmin, 'When brahmins meet they always ask one another whether or not they are brahmins.'

The Buddha: 'If you can say that you are a brahmin and that I am not, then I must remind you of Sāvitrī's mantra of three lines and twenty-four letters'.[2] (457)

4 The brahmin: 'But why have wise men of all kinds, whether religious, military or secular, always made so many offerings to the gods here in this world?'

The Buddha: 'If the person who receives the offering is at the moment of offering perfect in understanding, fulfilled and accomplished, then, I would say, the offering will be successful.' (458)

5 'This offering will certainly be successful, then', said the brahmin, 'for here in front of me is just such a man, a man perfect in understanding. If I hadn't seen you or someone like you, then I would have given the cake to some other person'. (459)

6 The Buddha: 'Since you are searching for something, brahmin, come here and ask about it. Perhaps you might find here an understanding that is clear, without anger or pain, or desire; one that is calm.' (460)

7 The brahmin: 'O Gotama, I very much like making offerings and I am anxious to make more. But I do not understand them. Can you teach me, and tell me what makes an offering effective?'

The Buddha: 'Listen carefully then, brahmin, and I will teach you about it. (461)

8 Do not ask about caste, but ask about conduct. Look at the flames of a fire. Where do they come from? From a piece of wood. In the same way a wise man may come from a low caste; through his firmness and moral restraint he becomes noble. (462)

9 This sense of truth quietens him, he learns self-control and, living a life of good conduct, he comes to complete understanding. This is where offerings should be given when offerings are due; this is where the brahmin, the man intent on positive action, gives offerings. (463)

10 There are wanderers who have given up homes and let sense pleasures go, who are practised in restraint and whose movement is as straight as a shuttle. This is where . . .[3] (464)

11 Those are those who are free from passion and with well composed faculties, who like the moon that has got free from the grip of Rāhu. This is where . . . (465)

12 There is no clinging to anything for these world-wanderers. They are always mindful and self-thoughts have been left behind. This is where . . . (466)

13 The wandering conqueror — who has let sense pleasures go — has seen where birth and death end. In the fullness of extinguishing he is cool like a lake: he is the One-Thus-Come [Tathāgata] and worthy of offerings. (467)

14 On a par with his equals, the even-minded, and beyond comparison with the uneven, the One-Thus-Come has limitless understanding. Nothing in this world or anywhere can pollute him: the One-Thus-Come is worthy of offerings. (468)

15 Pride and deceit do not exist; there is no trace of ignorance, of self-thoughts, of desire. Anger has been lost, and in the utter calm of full extinguishing the brahmin has removed the taint of grief. The One-Thus-Come is worthy of offerings. (469)

16 Resting places for the mind have gone. Grasping is no longer there at all. Clinging to nothing in this world or anywhere, the One-Thus-Come is worthy of offerings. (470)

17 He has crossed the stream, the mind is composed. In the perfection of knowledge he has realized the way things are. He is in his last body, and the passions are burnt out. The One-Thus-Come is worthy of offerings. (471)

18 The intoxication of being has been destroyed and eliminated, and so has abuse of speech; there is none of it. Liberated and fulfilled in every respect, the One-Thus-Come is worthy of offerings. (472)

19 He has shaken off ties, he is not tied down in any way, and there is never any pride, even when he is amongst proud people. He has come to understand where suffering begins and how far it goes. The One-Thus-Come is worthy of offerings. (473)

20 He seeks seclusion, not accepting desires and untouched by opinions. No objects of sense are clung to, none whatsoever: the One-Thus-Come is worthy of offerings. (474)

21 All ties of every description, thoroughly examined, are destroyed and eliminated; they have all gone. Calm in the freedom of extinguished attachment he is the One-Thus-Come and worthy of offerings. (475)

22 He sees the end of birth, the end of habit-chains. He has left completely the path of passion: pure, faultless, spotless, flawless, he is the One-Thus-Come and worthy of offerings. (476)

23 He does not see himself in terms of the self; poised, upright, firm, and free from desire, harshness and doubt, he is the One-Thus-Come and worthy of offerings. (477)

24 There is nothing in him that can lead to bewilderment; causes of ignorance are gone, there are none whatsoever. He perceives with insight all phenomena. He bears the last body. Full enlightenment is reached, ultimate and blissful, and purification of the person takes place. This is the One-Thus-Come and is worthy of offerings.' (478)

25 The brahmin: 'I have met a being who is complete in understanding; may my offering therefore be true! With Brahmā as my witness I ask the Buddha to accept me; may the Buddha enjoy these offerings?' (479)

26 The Buddha: 'Now, brahmin, I do not accept gifts earned by chanting texts; this is not the way with people of clear knowledge.

Enlightened beings reject what is earned by chanting texts, and while Truth exists this will always be the practice of Buddhas. (480)

27 You may attend upon a great sage who is perfect, who is passion-free and who has calmed anxiety with some other food and drink. That will be a field for the man intent on merit.' (481)

28 The brahmin: 'Very good, my Lord. But I should like to know to whom people like me should offer gifts. Tell me, in the light of your teaching, whom I should look for when I am making sacrifices?' (482)

29 – 30 The Buddha: 'Where there is no quarrel,
Where the mind is undisturbed,
Where there is freedom from lust,
Where lethargy is done away with,
Where passions are conquered,
Where birth and death are understood —
Here is the man of wisdom, the muni,
When a person like this is present at an offering. (483 – 4)

31 You should welcome him and honour him with food and drink, without any trace of a frown. This is how a gift will be effective.' (485)

32 The brahmin: 'Buddha, you are worthy of a gift, unsurpassable field of merit, and a recipient of sacrifice! What is given to your reverence is of immense fruit.' (486)

Then Sundarika-Bhāradvāja said to the Buddha: 'It is amazing, Venerable Gotama, it is wonderful, Venerable Gotama! Just as if one might raise what has been overturned, or reveal what has been hidden, or point out the way to him who has gone astray, or hold out a lamp in the dark so that those who have eyes may see objects, so likewise has the Truth been explained by Venerable Gotama in various ways. Therefore, I take refuge in him, his Dhamma and his Sangha. I wish to enter the homeless life and to receive the higher ordination near the Venerable Gotama.'

Then Sundarika-Bhāradvāja received ordination as a novice and received the higher ordination near the Buddha.

Later, by leading a secluded life, diligently, energetically and with a resolute will, in a short time he understood, experienced and attained that highest perfection of a noble life for which the sons of good families leave the household life, harmoniously, and take to the life of homelessness. Rebirth had been ended; a noble life had been led: what was to be done had been done and there was nothing else to be done in this earthly existence: Sundarika-Bhāradvāja had become one of the arahants.

Notes

1 *Pūraḷāsa* (Skt. *Puroḍāśa*): Sacrificial cake or brahminic oblation. *Carukañ ca pūvañ ca* (the lump of cane-sugar (saccharum) and cake). Sutta-Nipāta Commentary, p. 405. This is also called the *Sundarika-Bhāradvāja Sutta*.

2 The most celebrated hymn or prayer is addressed to Sāvitrī or the Sun. It is also called Gāyatrī. 'May we attain that excellent glory of Sāvitrī the god, that he may stimulate our thoughts.' (Ṛgveda, iii, 62, 10).

3 From 10 to 12 each stanza ends with the refrain, 'This is where offerings should be given when offerings are due; this is where the brahmin, the man intent on positive action, gives offerings.'

5. MĀGHA SUTTA

Māgha

(*Similar to the preceding Sutta*)

Thus have I heard: Once the Buddha was staying on Mount Vulture's Peak, near Rājagaha.

One day a young man, a brahmin called Māgha, came to see the Master. They greeted each other in the usual way and the young man sat down by the side of the Buddha.

'Gotama, sir', he said, 'I am a lay sponsor. I make donations, give financial support, presents, gifts, and such like. I am an approachable person and quite open to requests. The wealth I give away, I have made quite lawfully, and I distribute these lawful profits to one or two people, or sometimes to twenty or thirty people, or sometimes to a hundred or more. What I would like to know, sir, is whether it's worthwhile making all these gifts and offerings. Could you tell me if they produce merit for me?'

'Young man', said the Master, 'all these gifts and offerings you make are certainly worthwhile and they do produce great merit. It is the same for any man who makes donations and gives support, who stays approachable and open to requests, and who shares his lawful profits amongst one or two, or twenty or thirty, or a hundred people, or more. All these gifts will bring great merit to him.'

Then the young brahmin asked another question, and this time he spoke in verse:

1 'Gotama, sir', he said, 'you are a yellow-robed wanderer, a man without a home; you are a man who knows meaningful speech. Could you please answer this question for me: If a layman who is a charitable person, one from whom a gift may be expected makes an offering, desiring merit by giving food and drink to others, then offering to whom will his offering be pure?' (487)

2 'If this charitable layman', said the Master, 'is going to make an offering, or donate food and drink, and if he needs and wants to make merit, then to make the offering successful he must give it to someone who can receive a sacrifice. He must give it to someone who is giftworthy.' (488)

3 Then the brahmin asked the Buddha to tell him who these people were who could receive a sacrifice from charitable and well-intentioned laymen. 'Which people', asked the brahmin, 'are giftworthy?' (489)

4 And the Master replied:
'There are people who wander around in this world, without attachments, possessions, with nothing. They are whole and complete and they have control of the self.

When the time comes for giving, these are the people to give to. These are the people whom the well-intentioned brahmin should give to.[1] (490)

5 Those who have cut off the fetters and bonds, who are tamed, free, passionless and desireless. (491)

6 Those who are freed from all fetters, have tamed the wild and become free, free from the rage of passion and from desire. (492)

7 Getting rid of lust, hatred and delusion, they have eradicated the defilements and have perfected the religious life. (493)

8 There are people with no room for trickery or pride. They have no greed, no thoughts of 'I', no desire. (494)

9 They have gone across the ocean, for they did not fall prey to the thirst of craving. And so now they can live and move around without thoughts of 'I'. (495)

10 They do not have longings or yearnings for anything in the world. They have no longing to be something in this world and no longing to be in any other world. (496)

11 They have given up pleasure that is sense-based and they have perfect and fine self-control. They walk from one place to another without homes to return to and they move with directness, like a shuttle [pulling thread through a loom]. (497)

12 They are free from lust, their senses are well composed. They are free, slipped loose, like the moon easing free from the teeth of Rāhu [the Eclipse]. (498)

13 They are quietened and calm, with no passions or anger. They are not going anywhere in this world once they die: they have given up rebirth. (499)

14 They have given up birth and death with no remainder and they have gone beyond all doubt and uncertainty. (500)

15 They are islands unto themselves. They have nothing. They go from place to place and in every way they are free. (501)

16 They know precisely what this sentence means: "There will not be a rebirth: no more becoming. This is my last existence." (502)

17 In the enjoyment of meditation, in the fullness of knowledge and in the strength of mindfulness a person has full enlightenment and is a shelter for many. When the time comes for giving gifts, this is the person to give to: this is the person whom the well-intentioned brahmin gives to.' (503)

18 'Master', said Māgha, 'my question has certainly brougnt full rewards for me! You've explained to me what giftworthy means, and who these people are, for you know it as it really is — you have seen this in accordance with fact. (504)

19 But tell me one thing, Master. When a charitable and well-intentioned layman makes an offering or gives away food and drink, how should he do it to make the offering successful?' (505)

20 'Make your offering, Māgha', said the Master. 'As you make it be pleased in mind. Make your mind completely calm and contented. Focus and fill the offering-mind with the giving. From this secure position you can be free from ill-will. (506)

21 If you have no rush of passions and can get rid of ill-will, and if you develop the mind of boundless loving-kindness with constant care and alertness, night and day, then the loving-kindness will spread infinitely in each direction.' (507)

22 'O Master', said Māgha, 'tell me who can be pure, who can be free, who can be enlightened? How do you get to the Brahma-world on your own? O Master of wisdom, please tell me the answers! O Master, you yourself can witness that today I have seen Brahmā, for you are the same as Brahmā to us — it's true! O Master, Shining Light, please tell me how a man can get to the Brahma-world!' (508)

23 'Māgha', said the Master, I will say this to you: when the third of the three qualities of perfect giving is completed by giving to a giftworthy person, then, Māgha, the completed act of giving itself takes the giver, the man whose practice is giving, into the world of Brahma.' (509)

Then Māgha the young brahmin spoke in praise of the Master. It is amazing, Venerable Gotama, it is wonderful, Venerable Gotama! Just as if one might raise what has been overturned, or reveal what has been hidden, or point out the way to him who has gone astray, or hold out a lamp in the dark so that those who have eyes may see objects, so likewise has the Truth been explained by Venerable Gotama in various ways. Therefore, I take refuge in him, his Dhamma and his Sangha. May the Venerable Gotama accept me as a lay follower who henceforth has taken refuge in him for the rest of his life.'

Note

1 Repeated after vv. 5 – 16.

6. SABHIYA SUTTA

Sabhiya

A wandering ascetic questions the Buddha and the six contemporary teachers

Thus have I heard: Once the Buddha was staying in the Bamboo Grove by the squirrels' feeding-ground at Rājagaha. Now at about this time a wandering holy man was visited by a deva. The wanderer's name was Sabhiya and this deva had, in an earlier life, been a relative of his. The deva taught Sabhiya a list of questions that he should put to any holy man he met. 'If you find any priest or hermit who can answer them, then', said the deva, 'you should take that man as your teacher and commit yourself to a life of purity with him.'

So Sabhiya the wanderer learnt the questions by heart and set off to find all the great religious leaders of the time, all the famous teachers who had their own groups of followers and monks. He saw, successively, Purāṇa Kassapa, Makkhali Gosala, Ajita Kesa-kambali, Pakudha Kaccāyana, Sañjaya Belaṭṭhiputta and the Jain teacher Nātaputta [Mahāvīra], but none of them could answer his questions. Indeed, all of them got angry or uneasy when they saw that they had failed and started asking Sabhiya questions in return.

'I might as well give up and go back to easy living and a life of pleasure', thought Sabhiya. But then he thought of something else — there was one other holy man famous for his teaching and the number of his followers, a young man named Gotama. Why not ask him? 'But he', thought Sabhiya, 'is very young and has not been a holy man for long. How could he know more than the other, older teachers I have seen?' Another thought occurred to Sabhiya: a holy man should be respected for his power and his dignity, not for his age; so he decided after all to go and see the holy man Gotama.

Off he went on his pilgrimage until one day he came to Rājagaha. There, in the Bamboo Grove by the squirrels' feeding-ground, he found the Master. He greeted him politely, paid his respects and, after sitting down to one side, spoke in verse to the Master:

1 'I have come to you', said Sabhiya, 'full of confusion and doubt. I so much want to have these questions answered — please settle them for me once and for all and explain each answer to me one by one'. (510)

2 'You have come a long way, Sabhiya', said the Buddha, 'with these questions that you so much want to have answered. I will settle them for you once and for all and explain each answer to you one by one. (511)

3 Ask me whatever you want, Sabhiya, and I will explain it and clear up your confusion.'

Sabhiya thought, 'It is amazing, it is surprising; other recluses and brahmins did not even permit me to raise the questions, but the ascetic Gotama has at last permitted me to raise them.' He was glad, elated and encouraged and so he questioned the Buddha. (512)

4 'What, Master, must you do to be called a monk [bhikkhu]. What does it mean to be gentle? What is the meaning of restraint? And what does it mean to be a Buddha, to be enlightened? Please explain these four things to me, Master.' (513)

And this is what the Master told him:

5 'A monk, Sabhiya, is a person who has created a path for himself by which he has attained complete tranquility, overcoming doubt. He, having abandoned being and non-being, has perfected the religious life and has destroyed re-becoming. (514)

6 He is constantly equanimous and mindful. He does not harm anyone anywhere. A recluse is one who has crossed over [to Nibbāna]. He is unconfused. He has no evil traits. Such a one is gentle: he has crossed the ocean [of *Saṃsāra*]. (515)

7 He whose senses are cultivated in connection with the whole world, both internal and external; with penetrative understanding of this and the other world, the cultivated and restrained person awaits with equanimity the time of death. (516)

8 He who has scrutinized the entirety of thoughts and cyclic existence, consisting of both birth and death, the dustless, stainless, pure one who has attained the destruction of birth is called the Buddha [enlightened].' (517)

Sabhiya was thrilled to hear these words and went on to ask another set of questions.

9 'What do you have to do to be a brahmin? What does it mean to renounce, to be a holy man, a *samana*? What does it mean to be cleansed, and who can be called a hero? Please explain these things to me, Master.' (518)

And so the Master replied:

10 'A brahmin is a person who, having avoided all evil, is stainless, good, composed and poised. Overcoming the cycle of existence he has become perfect. He is unattached and steadfast. (519)

11 A holy man is a man who has calmed himself, is a man who has abandoned merit and demerit. Knowing this world and the other, he is dustless and has overcome birth and death. (520)

12 Washing away all evil connected with the whole world, both inner and outer, and with regard to men and gods he does not engage in conceptual thought. He is called the cleansed. (521)

13 Someone who lives in the world without doing wrong, someone who has untied all ties and chains, someone who does not hang on to anything anywhere, who is released, is called a steadfast hero.' (522)

Sabhiya, thrilled with these answers, went on to ask more questions:

14 'Who do enlightened men considered to be a world-winner? What does it mean to be skilled? What does it mean to be a man of understanding, and who is entitled to be called a wise man? Please, Master, explain these things to me.' (523)

And so the Master answered him:

15 'You ask what a world-winner is. There are three worlds: the world of men, the world of gods and the world of Brahma-beings.

A world-winner examines and understands all three. He has pulled up by the roots his links to these worlds and he is freed. This is the state called world-winner. (524)

16 You ask what skill is. There are three kinds of treasures or stores: those stocked by men, those stocked by gods and those stocked by Brahma-beings. The man of skill examines and understands all three. He has pulled up by the roots his links to these stocks and he is freed. This is the state called skill. (525)

17 A man of understanding is a man who has looked at his senses. He has understood how the senses work both in the mind and in the outside world. He sees with clarity, he has gone beyond "black and white" and is steadfast. (526)

18 And a man of wisdom? A wise man knows the Way of Distinguishing good from bad in connection with both the inner and the outer world. Both gods and men respect him: he has broken the chains and ropes.' (527)

Sabhiya, thrilled with these answers, went on to ask another set of questions:

19 'What do you have to achieve to be a man of knowledge? By what does one become an insightful person? How does one become an energetic man? And what does thoroughbred mean? Please explain these things to me, Master.' (528)

The Master told him this:

20 'When a man has looked at knowledge and understood all that is known to holy men and priests, then all the longings and yearnings for sensations disappear. Going beyond all knowledge he is a man of knowledge. (529)

21 Understanding the obsession of name and form [psycho-physical personality], the root of the disease both internal and external, he is freed from the ties to all roots of disease. Due to this reason he is called a steadfast, insightful person. (530)

22 Here he is free from all evil and has overcome the misery of hell, hence he is energetic. He is zealous, energetic, steadfast. (531)

23 You ask about the thoroughbred, the man of high birth: the thoroughbred snaps chains. There are internal and external chains and ropes and bonds — nobility means breaking them. It means pulling them up at the roots and being freed. This is the state called Thoroughbred.' (532)

Sabhiya, thrilled with these answers and full of joy, asked the Master another set of questions:

24 'What do you have to do to be a man of learning? What does it mean to be an *Ariya*, a man of noble birth? What is a man of perfect action? And who is entitled to the name of Wanderer? Please Master, explain these things to me.' (533)

And so the Master told him this:

25 'Having listened to all views he knows with wisdom whatever is blameworthy and blameless. He is victorious, freed and beyond confusion and disturbance. He is a man of learning. (534)

26 The wise one has cut off defilements and attachments. He does not go into lying in a womb. He has got rid of the three drives [greed, hate and delusion] and he does not enter into the mud of conceptual thinking. He is called the man of noble birth. (535)

27 Because a man of perfect action has lived and done correctly and with skill he grasps the Way Things Are. He has no attachment anywhere; he is freed, he has no [built-in] aversions: this is perfect action. (536)

28 And you ask about the Wanderer. When you see which actions hurt and when you leave those actions and are not in those actions, or above or below or beyond or between or anywhere near those actions, then you are a Wanderer. When you move from place to place and never lose your power to understand, then you are a Wanderer. When you lose your hating, wanting, delusion and pride, and when you end your sense of psychophysical individuality, then you have won success, and then you are a Wanderer.' (537)

Sabhiya the wanderer was thrilled at the Master's words. Full of joy and delight he got up from his seat and, with his hands folded and his shoulders bared, he spoke to the Master in verse:

29 'Master, Wise One', he said, 'you have done away with the [traditional] sixty-three argumentative theses, the conclusions of recluses which are mere conventions and speculative ideas. You have crossed over the flood and reached its end! (538)

30 You've gone to the very furthest point of suffering, and then you've gone beyond it. You, Master, are a Man of Worth; for you, I think, there are no more inner drives. You are glowing with understanding, radiating wisdom, finishing suffering and carrying me across! (539)

31 You saw what I was looking for, you knew what I was unsure of, and you carried me across! What mastery! What heights! — this is the ultimate in wisdom. I can give nothing but respect, nothing but honour to this power-house of gentleness, this brother of the sun! (540)

32 You have cleared up all my doubts with the eye of your perfect vision. So this is wisdom, this is Full Enlightenment! — this is what it's like to have nothing in your way. (541)

33 All worries have gone, disturbances cut out — and instead you have all that is calm, controlled, firm and precise. (542)

34 When you speak, the gods celebrate; when they hear you, they rejoice. You're a hero amongst heroes and a power amongst the strong! (543)

35 Nowhere in this world is there anyone like you — you are the best and the noblest being! I salute you and I honour you! (544)

36 You are the Buddha, the Enlightened. You are the Master, the Teacher. You are the Māra-conquering wisdom. You've cut out inner bias, inner weighing, and you have crossed over and you're taking us, all of us, with you. (545)

37 With the rebirth factors ended and the drives destroyed, you are at the end of clinging. You are a lion in the jungle, with nothing to frighten and nothing to fear. (546)

38 It's like a lotus flower on a lake! Good and evil roll off you, ineffective, like water drops off a lotus petal. Let me honour the feet of a conqueror: I am Sabhiya the worshipper at the feet of his teacher!' (547)

And so Sabhiya the wanderer bent down in respect at the feet of the Buddha and said: 'It is amazing, Venerable Gotama, it is wonderful, Venerable Gotama! Just as if one might raise what has been overturned, or reveal what has been hidden, or point out the way to him who has gone astray, or hold out a lamp in the dark so that those who have eyes may see objects, so likewise has the Truth been explained by Venerable Gotama in various ways. Therefore, I take refuge in him, his Dhamma and his Sangha. I wish to enter the homeless life and to receive the higher ordination near the Venerable Gotama.'

Then Sabhiya the wanderer received ordination as a novice and received the higher ordination near the Buddha.

Later, by leading a secluded life, diligently, energetically and with a resolute will, in a short time he understood, experienced and attained that highest perfection of a noble life for which the sons of good families leave the household life, harmoniously, and take to the life of homelessness. Rebirth had been ended; a noble life had been led: what was to be done had been done and there was nothing else to be done in this earthly existence: Sabhiya the wanderer had become one of the arahants.

7. SELA SUTTA

Sela

The Buddha convinces Sela and company of his enlightenment

Thus have I heard: Once the Buddha was travelling in the company of over 1,250 monks and reached a market town called Āpaṇa in Aṅguttarāpa.

An ascetic with matted hair called Keṇiya heard thus: that the venerable Gotama, a descendant of the Sākyan clan, who had renounced his family, had arrived at Āpana. And he had also heard these words of praise: 'That Blessed One is such since he is accomplished, fully-enlightened, endowed with wisdom and conduct, sublime, the knower of worlds, the incomparable leader of men to be tamed, the teacher of gods and men, enlightened and glorious.' He (the Buddha) himself having realized the Truth (Dhamma) makes it known to the world of men and gods including ascetics and brahmins. He teaches the Truth which is good in the beginning, in the middle and at the end, full of meaning, rich in words and wholly complete. He teaches a perfect, pure life. Good, indeed, is the sight of such saints!

Then the ascetic Keṇiya went to see the Buddha and after exchanging greetings sat on one side. The Buddha made him very happy with a discourse whereupon Keṇiya invited the Buddha together with his retinue of monks for lunch on the following day. However, the Buddha warned him of the large number of monks in his company and alluded to Keṇiya's close friendship with the brahmins. Undeterred, Keṇiya persisted with his invitation and on the third occasion of asking, the Buddha assented to his request by keeping silent. Thereupon Keṇiya returned to his hermitage and solicited the assistance of his friends, servants and relations to help arrange the almsgiving. They all worked in various capacities, Keṇiya himself erecting a circular pavilion.

At that time a brahmin called Sela lived in Āpaṇa. He was well versed in the three Vedas, vocabulary, prosody, rhetoric, etymology, history, versed in metre, a grammarian, one not deficient in popular controversy and the science of physiognomy. He taught 300 young men. Since he was on friendly terms with Keṇiya, he visited his hermitage along with his pupils. Seeing the brisk preparations going on there he remarked to Keṇiya: 'Will there be a marriage of a son or daughter, is a great sacrifice about to take place, or has King Bimbisāra of Magadha been invited for lunch tomorrow together with his large army?'

Keṇiya replied: 'Nothing of that kind is going on here. Yet a great sacrifice of mine is approaching; the ascetic Gotama the Buddha with his disciples has been invited for lunch tomorrow.' 'Do you say that he is a Buddha!' 'Yes, I do.'

Then this thought occurred to Sela: 'The word "Buddha" is, indeed, rare. But in our Vedas the thirty-two signs of a great man are found. There are but two conditions to such a person and none other: if he leads a household life he will become a king, an emperor, a just ruler. If, however, he renounces the household for the homeless life he will become a saint, a fully-enlightened one, one who has removed the covering of the defilements.' 'O Keṇiya, where does the Buddha dwell now?' 'Where, O Sela, lies the forest belt.'

Then Sela, together with his 300 disciples, approached the Buddha and, noticing the signs of a great man on his body, praised him in a suitable verse:

1 O Buddha, you have a perfect body, you are resplendent, well-born, handsome, of golden colour; you have white teeth and you are energetic. (548)

2 If there be any signs of a man who is well-born, all those signs of a great man are on your body. (549)

3 You have bright eyes, a handsome countenance; you are great, straight, majestic; you shine like the sun in the midst of the assembly of monks. (550)

4 You are a monk of lovely appearance; you have a skin like gold; what advantage can there be in being an ascetic when you are possessed of such a splendid complexion? (551)

5 You deserve to be a king, an emperor, the lord of chariots, whose conquests reach to the limits of the four seas, lord of the Jambu grove [i.e. India]. (552)

6 Warrior and wealthy kings are devoted to you; O Gotama, exercise your royal power as a king of kings, a chief of men! (553)

The Buddha:

7 I am a king, O Sela, supreme king of the Teaching of Truth; I turn the wheel by pure-means — this wheel is irresistible. (554)

Sela:

8 You maintain that you are a fully-enlightened one, a king of Truth; O Gotama, you say, 'I turn the wheel by pure means'. (555)

9 Who is your general, who is your disciple? Who is the follower of the teacher? Who, hereafter, will turn the wheel of Truth turned by you? (556)

The Buddha:

10 O Sela, Sāriputta will hereafter turn the incomparable wheel of Truth turned by me; he walks after the Tathāgata. (557)

11 What is to be known is known by me; what is to be cultivated is cultivated by me; what is to be destroyed has been destroyed by me. Therefore, O brahmin, I am the Buddha. (558)

12 O brahmin, subdue your doubts about me, have confidence in me! Rare is it to obtain the sight of fully-enlightened ones. (559)

13 O brahmin, of those whose manifestation is rare for you to see, I am a representative, an incomparable physician. (560)

14 Pre-eminent, matchless, the vanquisher of Māra and his army, having brought under subjection all enemies I rejoice, secure from all directions. (561)

Sela:

15 O friends, pay attention to what the seeing one says! He is a physician, a great hero, and roars like a lion in the forest. (562)

16 Having seen him, pre-eminent, matchless, the vanquisher of Māra and his army, who cannot be overcome even if he be of black origin?[1] (563)

17 He who wishes, let him follow me; he who does not wish let him go away, for I shall now enter the Order under the excellent, wise one. (564)

The followers of Sela:

18 If the Dispensation of the fully-enlightened one pleases you, we also shall enter the Order under the excellent, wise one! (565)

Sela:

19 These 300 brahmins, with clasped hands, state: 'We will practise the pure life under the accomplished one'. (566)

The Buddha:

20 Sela, the pure life is well proclaimed by me: visible here and now; affording result without delay; it is not in vain that one may become a monk whereby one may train himself diligently. (567)

Then the brahmin Sela together with his assembly entered the Order and received the higher ordination under the Buddha.

Meanwhile, the ascetic Keṇiya informed the Buddha that lunch was ready. Consequently he went to Keṇiya's hermitage together with his assembly of monks where they were served with sumptuous food. On completion of the meal, the Buddha delighted Keṇiya with these words:

21 'The principal item in the sacrifice is fire; the principal figure in the hymns is Sāvitri; the king is the principal amongst men; and, amongst rivers, the sea is principal. (568)

22 Amongst the planets the moon is the principal; amongst burning objects the sun is principal: amongst those who make offerings, wishing for merit, the community of monks indeed is principal.' (569)

Then the Buddha, having delighted Keṇiya with these verses, went away. Then the venerable Sela together with his assembly retired to a solitary place and led such a strenuous, ardent and energetic existence that, within a short time, in this present life, by his own understanding, ascertained and possessed himself of that highest perfection of a pure life for the sake of which men of good family renounce their home for homelessness. Becoming was destroyed; a pure life had been led; what had to be done was done and there was nothing else to be done in this existence. Thus the Venerable Sela together with his assembly became arahants. Thereafter, they went to the Buddha and after making salutation addressed him in verse:

23 'On the eighth day previous to this we took refuge in you; O Venerable Sir, within seven nights we were trained in your Dispensation. (570)

24 You are the Buddha; you are the teacher; you are the muni who conquered Māra; after cutting off latent inclinations you crossed over the stream of existence and took over these beings to the other shore. (571)

25 The objects of attachment have been overcome by you; the influxes have been destroyed by you: you are a lion not seizing on "clinging"; you have left behind fear and terror. (572)

26 These 300 monks stand here with clasped hands; O hero, stretch out your feet and let the Nāgas[2] worship the teacher's feet!' (573)

Notes

1 The brahmin's claim is that he alone is of a bright colour (*varṇa*) whilst the remaining three divisions of (Hindu) society-warrior (kṣatriya), tradesman (vaiśya) and labourer (śudra) — are black in complexion. The Buddha was born in the warrior caste and hence the appellation, 'black origin' (*kaṇābhiịāliko*).

2 A kind of demon gifted with miraculous powers. In this instance the term is used figuratively in the sense of 'saints', 'chiefs' or 'liberated ones'.

8. SALLA SUTTA

The Dart

A recollection on death

1 Life is unpredictable and uncertain in this world. Life here is difficult, short and bound up with suffering. (574)

2 A being, once born, is going to die, and there is no way out of this. When old age arrives, or some other cause, then there is death. This is the way it is with living beings. (575)

3 When fruits become ripe, they may fall in the early morning. In just the same way a being, once born, may die at any moment. (576)

4 Just as the clay pots made by the potter tend to end up being shattered, so is it with the life of mortals. (577)

5 Both the young and the old, whether they are foolish or wise, are going to be trapped by death. All beings move towards death. (578)

6 They are overcome by death. They go to the other world. And then not even a father can save his son, or a family their relatives. (579)

7 Look: while relatives are watching, tearful and groaning, men are carried off one by one, like cattle being led to the slaughter. (580)

8 So death and ageing are endemic to the world. Therefore the wise do not grieve seeing the nature of the world. (581)

9 You cannot know his path as to where he has come from, or where he is going to. So it makes no sense to grieve for him. (582)

10 The man who grieves gains nothing. He is doing no more than a foolish man who is trying to hurt himself. If a wise man does it, it is the same for him. (583)

11 Peace of mind cannot come from weeping and wailing. On the contrary, it will lead to more suffering and greater pain. (584)

12 The mourner will become pale and thin. He is doing violence to himself, and still he cannot keep the dead alive; his mourning is pointless. (585)

13 The man who cannot leave his sorrow behind him only travels further into pain. His mourning makes him a slave to sorrow. (586)

14 Look at beings who are facing death, who are living out the results of their previous deeds; people are terrified when they see that they are trapped by death. (587)

15 What people expect to happen is always different from what actually happens. From this comes great disappointment; this is the way the world works. (588)

16 A man may live for a hundred years, or even more, but in the end he is separated from his relatives, and he too leaves life in this world. (589)

17 So we can listen and learn from the noble man as he gives up his grief. When he sees that someone has passed away and lived out their life, he says 'he will not be seen by me again'. (590)

18 When a house is burning, the fire is put out by water. In the same way the wise man, skilful, learned and self-reliant, extinguishes sorrow as soon as it arises in him. It is like the wind blowing away a tuft of cotton. (591)

19 The person who is searching for his own happiness should pull out the dart that he has stuck in himself, the arrow-head of grieving, of desiring, of despair. (592)

20 The man who has taken out the dart, who has no clinging, who has obtained peace of mind, passed beyond all grief, this man, free from grief, is still. (593)

9. VĀSEṬṬHA SUTTA

Vāseṭṭha

The correct definition of 'brahmin'

Thus have I heard: Once the Buddha was staying in the forest of Icchānaṅgala. Many brahmins were staying there too, famous men like Cañkī, Tārukkha, Pokkharasāti, Jāṇussoṇi and Todeyya — all well-known, erudite and wealthy brahmins.

Amongst these men were two young brahmins, one called Vāseṭṭha and the other Bhāradvāja. Now, one day, as these two young men were walking up and down, they started a conversation regarding the factors that make one a brahmin.

Bhāradvāja said: 'It's to do with one's family. If one's family background is pure, and there has been no intermarriage with other castes for seven generations back, on either one's mother's or one's father's side, then one is a brahmin.'

But Vāseṭṭha said: 'If one's actions are good and duties are observed, then one is a brahmin.'

Bhāradvāja stuck to his theory and Vāseṭṭha stuck to his: neither could convince the other that he was right. So Vāseṭṭha suggested that they go and ask someone else's advice. 'Listen', he said to Bhāradvāja, 'There is a hermit called Gotama, a prince of the Sākyas, who has renounced his family and of whom it is said: "That Blessed One is such since he is accomplished, fully-enlightened, endowed with wisdom and conduct, sublime, the knower of worlds, the incomparable leader of men to be tamed, the teacher of gods and men, enlightened and glorious". He (the Buddha) himself having realized the Truth (Dhamma) makes it known to the world of men and gods including ascetics and brahmins. He teaches the Truth which is good in the beginning, in the middle and at the end, full of meaning, rich in words and wholly complete. He teaches a perfect, pure life. Good, indeed, is the sight of such saints!'

'Well, Bhāradvāja', said Vāseṭṭha, 'let's go to this man Gotama, and ask him to clear up this question and we will take it as the recluse Gotama explains it.'

'Very well', said Bhāradvāja, 'Let's go.' So the two young men went off to look for this Master. When they found him they greeted him politely and sat down on one side. Then Vāseṭṭha spoke to the Master in these words:

1 'Sir, we are both students of the orthodox teachings and we are both recognized and accepted as experts in the study of the Vedas. My teacher is Pokkharasāti, and my friend here studies with Tārukkha. (594)

2 We've studied all the commentaries on the three Vedas, and we're qualified to teach the subjects of metre, grammar and chanting. (595)

3 But even so, Gotama, there is one question about which we are in disagreement, namely, the importance of heredity. Bhāradvāja insists that a man is a brahmin because he is born as one, but I am sure that it's what a man does that counts. We want you, who have vision, to know about this argument. (596)

4 Because we can't settle it between ourselves, we have come to ask you about it. We've heard that you are called the fully-enlightened one. (597)

5 You are treated with respect by men — they fold their hands when they see you in the same way they go forth to respect the waxing moon. (598)

6 You are the eye of the world, Gotama, so we ask you to look at this question — what is it that makes a man a brahmin? Is it by birth or is it by what he does? We can't work it out, Gotama, so please explain it to us and tell us what a brahmin is.' (599)

7 The Buddha answered Vāseṭṭha in these words:
'I shall explain to you in proper order and in accordance with the fact the different kinds of living things, since there are diverse species. (600)

8 If you look at trees or grass, although they may not be conscious of it, there are lots of different kinds and species. There are divergent species. (601)

9 Then there are insects, large ones like moths and small ones like ants: with these creatures too you can see that they are of different kinds and species. (602)

10 And in four-footed animals, whatever the size, you can see that they are of different kinds and species. (603)

11 Now look at the creatures that crawl on their bellies, the reptiles and the snakes — you can see that they are of different kinds and species. (604)

12 – 13 Look at the fish and water life — look at birds and the breeds that fly — you can see that they are of different kinds and species. (605 – 6)

14 There is not among men different kinds and species in the manner that they are found among other species. (607)

15 Unlike in other species there is not among men differences in kind or species with regard to their eyes, ears, mouths, noses, lips, eyebrows and even their hair — all are the same type. (608)

16 From the neck to the groin, from the shoulder to the hip, from the back to the chest — it is all of one kind with men. (609)

17 Hands, feet, fingers, nails, calves and thighs are all standard, and so are the features of voice and of colour. Unlike other creatures, men do not have characteristics which distinguished them at birth. (610)

18 They do not have the variety of inherited features that other creatures have. In fact, in the case of humans, differences are differences only by convention.[1] (611)

19 For example, Vāseṭṭha, if a man keeps cows and lives off their produce, then we know that he is a farmer — we do not call him a brahmin. (612)

20 Similarly, when a man lives by a particular craft, then we know he is a craftsman — we do not call him a brahmin. (613)

21 If he supports himself by trading then we know he is a merchant not a brahmin. (614)

22 When a man gets paid for serving other people, then we call him a servant rather than a brahmin. (615)

23 A man who lives by taking other people's things is known as a thief rather than a brahmin. (616)

24 And a bowman who sells his skill is known as a soldier — we do not call him a brahmin. (617)

25 A man whose work is performing rites and ceremonies is known as a priest and not as a brahmin. (618)

26 And the man who lives off the produce of countries and villages is known as a landlord or a king — we do not call him a brahmin. (619)

27 I do not call a man a brahmin because of his mother or because of his breeding. Just because a man is entitled to be called "Sir", it does not mean that he is free from habit and attachment. He who is free from attachment, he who is free from grasping is the person I call a brahmin. (620)

28 When all the chains are shattered, when there is no more agitation, and a man has freed himself and thrown off his shackles — that is the person I call a brahmin. (621)

29 He who has cut off the strap [of ignorance] and harness [of false views], who has removed obstacles and is enlightened, is one I call a brahmin. (622)

30 He who, without getting annoyed, endures insults and violence, whose strength and army is endurance, is one I call a brahmin. (623)

31 There is no anger and there is no ignorance — there is only strength of restraint and the power of pure action. So there is no habitual repetition, no rebirth. This is what I call [being] a brahmin. (624)

32 Like a water drop on a lotus leaf, a mustard seed on the top of a needle, sense-desires roll off and leave no trace in him. It is such a person I call a brahmin. (625)

33 Losing weight and dropping a chain — here, right here in this world, he can see how even suffering has an end. This is whom I call a brahmin. (626)

34 One who is deep in wisdom, wise, proficient in what the right or the wrong path is, who has reached the ultimate goal, is one I call a brahmin. (627)

35 No props, no dependency, no need to mix with other people, whether property owners or wandering monks — the minimum being good enough; this is what "brahmin" means. (628)

36 To lay down the weapons of violence, to stop killing any being, to stop causing others to kill any being; this is what "brahmin" means. (629)

37 He who shows no anger towards those who are angry, peaceful towards those who are violent, not grasping among those who are bent on grasping, is one I call a brahmin. (630)

38 He whose wanting, hating, pride and envy have dropped away, like the mustard seed which has rolled off the needle top, is one I call a brahmin. (631)

39 He who speaks words which are not harsh and words which are meaningful and true, words which do not rouse another's anger, is one I call a brahmin. (632)

40 No possessions, no things have been appropriated, whatever the size, quantity or value; this is what "brahmin" means. (633)

41 No expectations, not a hankering for this world or for any other: he is untied, released; this is what "brahmin" means. (634)

42 An absence of wanting — questions and doubts disappear in knowledge and he plunges into the absence of death; this is what "brahmin" means. (635)

43 He who has gone beyond the [impurity of both] merit and demerit, who is free from grief and defilement and is pure; this is what "brahmin" means. (636)

44 The clear, calm, stainless, moonlike quality where the shackles of constant becomings are cut and thrown away; this is what "brahmin" means. (637)

45 He who has gone beyond the rough and dangerous road of cyclic existence and delusion, who has crossed over and gone beyond, the contemplative, passionless and doubt-free, one who is calmed without grasping, is one I call a brahmin. (638)

46 Sense pleasures have gone — he lets them go for the life of a wanderer without a home. The sensual pleasure of constant becoming has gone, thrown away; this is what "brahmin" means. (639)

47 Craving-demandings have gone — he lets them go for the life of a wanderer without a home. The hankering after constant becomings has gone, thrown away; this is what "brahmin" means. (640)

48 The dead-weight on the backs of men, the loads that weigh down even gods — all these burdens are discarded, thrown off and overcome: he is untied from the yoke, released. This is what "brahmin" means. (641)

49 Avoiding delight and aversion, he is cooled and free from the bases [that lead to rebirth]. He is a hero who has overcome all the worlds and is one I call a brahmin. (642)

50 He who has fully comprehended how beings come to be and how they cease to be, is unattached, faring rightly and enlightened, is one I call a brahmin. (643)

51 He whose destiny cannot be known by gods and human beings, the person who has eradicated the passions, a worthy one, is one I call a brahmin. (644)

52 As for possessions, he has nothing — nothing in the past, nothing in the future, nothing in the present. He does not hold on to anything at all; freed from clinging, this is what I call a brahmin. (645)

53 A hero — a man of greatness, of prominence, of wisdom, a man of fearlessness and victory. Non-attached; washed [in the waters of wisdom]; enlightened. This is what I call a brahmin. (646)

54 He knows his earlier lives, he has seen the other forms of life, the woeful states and the happy states. This is the attainment:

reaching the end of the chain-links of births. This is what I call a brahmin. (647)

55 So what of all these titles, names and races? They are mere worldly conventions. They have come into being by common consent. (648)

56 This false belief has been deeply ingrained in the minds of the ignorant for a long time and [still] these ignorant ones say to us: "One becomes a brahmin by birth." (649)

57 [On the contrary,] no one is *born* a brahmin; no one is *born* a non-brahmin. A brahmin is a brahmin because of what he *does*; a man who is not a brahmin is not a brahmin because of what he *does*. (650)

58 A farmer is a farmer because of what he does and a craftsman is a craftsman because of what he does. (651)

59 A merchant, a servant, a thief, a soldier, a priest or a king: each of them is what he is because of what he does. (652)

60 So the wise men see action as it has really come to be. They are proficient in the fruits of action and they are seers of dependent origination. (653)

61 The world exists because of causal actions, all things are produced by causal actions and all beings are governed and bound by causal actions. They are fixed like the rolling wheel of a cart, fixed by the pin of its axle shaft. (654)

62 A brahmin is as a result of self-restraint, wholesome living and self-control. This is the essence of Brahmin. (655)

63 So, Vāseṭṭha, let this be clear: there are people who are wise and experienced in all the three areas of knowledge [i.e. the Vedas], who are calm and have finished with the chain-links of repeated becoming. These people should be known like Brahmā or Indra.' (656)

Then Vāseṭṭha and Bhāradvāja said to the Buddha: 'It is amazing, Venerable Gotama, it is wonderful, Venerable Gotama! Just as if one might raise what has been overturned, or reveal what has been hidden, or point out the way to him who has gone astray, or hold out a lamp in the dark so that those who have eyes may see objects, so likewise has the Truth been explained by Venerable Gotama in various ways. Therefore, we take refuge in him, his Dhamma and his Sangha. May the Venerable Gotama accept us as lay followers who henceforth have taken refuge in him for the rest of their lives.'

Note

1 It should be borne in mind that, when describing the physical characteristics of human beings, the Buddha only referred to his fellow Indians of the north-east and central parts of the subcontinent.

The Buddha is here referring to *observable* differences from his own personal experience and later explains that actions (*kamma*) and behaviour are the keys to perfection and enlightenment. The natural corollary of rebirth, however, can lead to people being born in 'high' or 'low' estates — i.e. environments that can either encourage or retard spiritual (or even material) growth. Thus, although the *potentiality* for understanding is present in every person, *kamma* ensures a perpetual inequality of results.

It would, therefore, be irrelevant to quote this passage out of context in any debate on 'racial equality', as was done by K. N. Jayatilleke and G. P. Malalasekera in their essay, *Buddhism and the Race Question* (UNESCO, Paris, 1958; repr. BPS, Kandy 1974). For a commonsense Buddhist approach to this issue see Philip Eden *Human Progress: Reality or Illusion?* (BPS 1974).

10. KOKĀLIKA SUTTA

Kokālika

The dire consequences of unwholesome speech

Once, when the Buddha was staying in the Jetavana Monastery at Sāvaṭṭhi, a monk called Kokālika came up to him and said:

'Sir, Sāriputta and Moggallāna are full of unwholesome desires. They have been quite taken over by unwholesome desires.'

The Buddha answered:

'Kokālika, don't say such a thing! Have confidence in your mind as far as they are concerned; Sāriputta and Moggallāna are well behaved.'

But Kokālika repeated his accusation against the two disciples. The Buddha replied as before, but the monk again insulted the disciples in the same way. For a third time he was asked by the Buddha not to do so. Then Kokālika, making a deep bow to the Buddha, got up and went away.

He had only gone a short way when he started to feel ill. His whole body came out in boils, boils the size of mustard seeds. These boils began to swell, growing bit by bit until they were as large as peas. Then they grew as large as beans, as eggs, as crab apples and as quinces. At this point they burst open, oozing pus and blood. From the illness Kokālika died and, as a result of the ill-will that he had shown, he was reborn in one of the states of misery which is known as the Paduma or Lotus.

Towards the end of that night the Brahmā Sahampati came to the Buddha and told him how Kokālika had died, and how his ill-will had caused rebirth to take place in the Paduma. Early next morning the Buddha called all the monks together to explain what he had told him about Kokālika's death: 'Monks, the life of a being in the Paduma state lasts so long that we can hardly describe it in numbers. Kokālika has taken birth there because of the ill-will he had for Sāriputta and Moggallāna.'

And, as Teacher, the Buddha went on to say this:

1 A person that is born is born with an axe in his mouth. He whose speech is unwholesome cuts himself with this axe. (657)

2 When a man praises someone who should be blamed, or attacks someone worthy of praise, then this man is accumulating evil with his mouth and this evil will not lead to happiness. (658)

3 It is little harm if one loses money in gambling with dice, even losing everything, including oneself; but if one bears ill-will towards well-conducted ones it is greater harm indeed. (659)

4 Insulting men of real worth, bearing ill-will in thought and speech, leads to aeons upon aeons in the states of misery. (660)

5 Lying leads to these states. Doing something and then saying, 'I didn't do it' — this is the same as lying. In terms of death and rebirth both actions are equivalent: at death you must face the consequences of unwholesome actions. (661)

6 When a man attacks someome who is peaceful, pure and uncorrupted, then the attack turns back on the foolish man who started it as dust thrown against the wind. (662)

7 The person who has a greedy disposition insults others with words. He is faithless, greedy, miserly and slanderous. (663)

8 If you are a man like this, untrue and unworthy, slanderous, evil and misbehaved, mean, bad, you had better not talk too much or else you will come to a state of misery! (664)

9 You are spreading pollution when you act like this. It is an insult to men who do good, and it is a polluted action in itself. If you accumulate actions like this you will fall into the pool of misery-states. (665)

10 Why is this? It is because the things that men do just do not disappear into the past. They will come back to us, they will return to their maker. A man whose actions are polluted is foolish: in time he will feel the pain of it himself. (666)

11 The pain he will feel will be like the pain of iron bars that are thrashing him and iron stakes that are piercing him. In a state like that, what he eats feels like red-hot balls of iron. (667)

12 Nothing there is said that is not hard and painful. There are no pleasing words of consolation, nothing offers escape for the sufferers in this state, this state where the world is a furnace, where even a bed is of red-hot ashes. (668)

13 Tangled up in nets, crushed by hammer-blows, they are immersed in thick darkness stretching out on all sides. (669)

14 Then they find themselves in a cauldron, burning and boiling, bubbling up and down in the heat of the furnace, heaving their bodies around. (670)

15 The man of unwholesome deeds is in this state, stewing and boiling in blood and rotten flesh. Wherever he moves to he rots from the touch of this putrid mash. (671)

16 Then the man of unwholesome deeds boils in water infested with worms. He cannot stay still — the boiling pots, round and smooth like bowls, have no surfaces which he can get hold of. (672)

17 Then he is in the jungle of sword blades, limbs mangled and hacked, the tongue hauled by hooks, the body beaten and slashed. (673)

18 Then he is in Vetaraṇī, a watery state difficult to get through, with its two streams that cut like razors. The poor beings fall into it, living out their unwholesome deeds of the past. (674)

19 Gnawed by hungry jackals, ravens and black dogs, and speckled vultures and crows, the sufferers groan. (675)

20 Such a state is experienced by the man of unwholesome deeds. It is a state of absolute suffering. So a sensible person in this world is as energetic and mindful as he can be. (676)

21 The Paduma state lasts a long time. The experts work out its length in terms of the number of cartloads of sesame seeds that would be emptied if one seed were removed every hundred years. They say the cartloads would number five thousand one hundred and twenty million. (677)

22 And as long as the misery-states are called miserable by people in this world, for so long will people have to go on living through those states.

Take care therefore and with pure, wholesome and friendly qualities constantly watch the movements of mind and the movements of speech. (678)

11. NĀLAKA SUTTA

Nālaka

The birth of the future Buddha and a description of the qualities of enlightenment

1 One day, during the afternoon siesta, the sage Asita noticed that the thirty gods had all gathered together. Full of joy and overflowing with praises to Indra, they were dressed in the purest white and waved their robes and banners with delight. (679)

2 Seeing all this excitement, Asita respectfully asked the gods what it was that they were celebrating. 'Why are you all so happy and joyful?' he asked, 'What's all this waving and whirling of banners for? (680)

3 I've never seen such excitement as this, not even when the gods won their battle against the Asuras. What can they have seen now? It must be something wonderful for there to be all this rejoicing. (681)

4 They are singing and shouting, playing music, dancing around, clapping and waving — tell me why, you people from thc top of Mount Meru! Please answer my qucstions, put my mind at rest!' (682)

5 'In a village called Lumbinī, in the Sākyan country', answered the gods, 'a bodhisatta has been born! A being set on Buddhahood has been born, a superlative being without comparison, a precious pearl of the health and goodness of the human world. That's why we're so glad, so excited, so pleased. (683)

6 Of all beings this onc is perfect, this man is the pinnacle, the ultimate, the hero of creatures! This is the man who, from the forest of the Masters, will set the wheel of Teaching turning — the roar of the lion, King of Beasts!' (684)

7 When he heard this news, Asita left the Tusita heaven and went straight to the palace of Suddhodana, King of the Sākyas. There, when he had sat down, he said to the Sākyas: 'Where is the prince? I would like to see him.' (685)

8 So they took the hermit Asita, the 'Unattached', as he was called, and showed him the new-born prince. He was shining, glowing and beautiful. It was like seeing molten gold in the hands of a master craftsman as he takes it out of the furnace. (686)

9 To see the prince was to see brightness — the brightness of the flames of a fire; the brightness of the star constellations crossing the night sky; the brightness and clarity of the autumn sun shining on a cloudless day. It was a sight that filled the hermit with joy, and he experienced great delight. (687)

10 In the sky above, invisible beings were holding up a vast canopy out in circles from its centre and stretched over a thousand spokes. Other gods waved yak-tailed fans on golden stems, and these gods too were invisible. (688)

11 The long-haired sage, the 'Dark Splendour', as he was called, looked at the baby lying on the orange clothes, shining like a golden coin, with the white sunshade held up above him. With great joy he picked him up. (689)

12 Now the lion of the Sākyas was in the arms of a man who had waited for him, a man who could recognize all the signs on his body — a man who now, filled with delight, raised his voice to say these words: 'There is nothing to compare with this: this is the ultimate, this is the perfect man!' (690)

13 Just then the hermit remembered that he was going to die quite soon — and he felt so sad at this that he began to cry. The Sākyas asked him why he was crying: 'Is the prince in some danger?' they asked. (691)

14 To settle their worries, the sage explained to them why he felt sad. 'No', he said, 'there will not be any danger or threat to the prince's life, as far as I can see. In fact, for him there won't be any obstacles at all. There couldn't be for him; he is not an ordinary being. [Listen carefully:] (692)

15 This prince will come to the fulfilment of perfect Englightenment; this prince of supremely pure vision will start turning the wheel of Truth out of compassion for the well-being of many. The religious life will be fully expounded. (693)

16 But for me there is a grain of sadness and pain in this. For I will not live much longer now and during his life I shall die. So I won't be able to see this man of such unparalleled strength teaching how things are — and that's the only reason that I felt sad.' (694)

17 The Sākyas were thrilled to hear what he said, and he left them, went out from the inner rooms of the palace and set out to follow the practices of a pure and virtuous life. But as he was leaving he began to think of his nephew, Nālaka, and, full of compassion, he stopped to tell him about this man of unequalled strength and his teaching. (695)

18 'One day', he said to his nephew, 'You will hear someone talking about "a Buddha". You will hear of a man who has reached full enlightenment by following the correct path. When you hear this, go and find out all the details of this teaching — go and live with this Master, this Lord, and follow the practices of a pure life.' (696)

19 And Nālaka, helped by the merit he had accumulated by many years of good and wholesome actions, remained alert and restrained, always moderating the play of his senses, looking forward to the appearance of this conquering hero. (697)

20 In time, the news did come: the Buddha started to turn the teaching wheel. On Asita's advice Nālaka went off to find this noble sage and, having done so, asked the man of wisdom about the highest wisdom: (698)

(*The end of the verses of the prologue*)

21 'What Asita told me many years before has turned out true', said Nālaka, 'I can see that now. You, Gotama, have reached the perfection of all things; may I now put a question to you, Master? (699)

22 I have lived for sometime as a wanderer and now I would like to live as a monk, so please, answer this question for me: What is the highest wisdom state?' (700)

23 And the sublime Master replied, 'I will explain the wisdom state to you, a state which is hard to get and hard to put into effect. Come, be alert and full of effort. (701)

24 Develop the mind of equilibrium. You will always be getting praise and blame, but do not let either affect the poise of the mind: follow the calmness, the absence of pride. (702)

25 Forms, both high and low come across, like tongues of flame from a log. Women tempt the sage but you should not develop the desire for them. (703)

26 – 27 Being free from sensuous union, without aversion or attachment towards beings, however weak or strong they may be, comparing oneself to others in such terms as "Just as I am so are they, just as they are so am I'', he should neither kill nor cause others to kill. (704–5)

28 The impulse ''I want'' and the impulse ''I'll have'' — lose them! That is where most people get stuck — without those, you can use your eyes to guide you through this suffering state. (706)

29 Eating little and moderate in food, with few wants and free from greed, he is unafflicted by wants. He is desireless and calmed. (707)

30 [This is the pattern that the man of wisdom follows.] He goes round collecting gifts for his meals, and then he goes off to the edge of the woods and sits down under a tree. (708)

31 He applies himself to meditation practice. With his skill in this practice he can find it pleasurable. He can make himself joyful, living under a tree on the edge of the wood, meditating. (709)

32 He spends the night like this and in the morning sets off for the village. He does not get distracted, he does not get excited by the gifts and invitations that people offer him there. (710)

33 Once he has reached the village he does not rush from door to door, and when he is begging for food he does not talk about it or pass any hints. (711)

34 He simply says, ''This is what I've been given: that's good'', or ''I haven't been given anything: that's fine''. With this attitude towards begging he can return undisturbed to the tree. (712)

35 So he wanders around with begging bowl in hand, although he is not dumb he seems to be dumb. He accepts even the smallest gift or the slightest giver without scorn and without pride. (713)

36 The methods, both quick and slow, by which Nibbāna may be discerned have indeed been expounded by the ascetic Gotama. It [Nibbāna] is never discerned twice; this perceiving of the beyond is realized gradually [by the four stages[1]]. (714)

37 When a person is desireless, when a monk has extinguished the river of becomings, when he has given up all the activities of duty and obligation — he ''ought to'' and ''ought not to'' — then the fever is past.' (715)

38 'Yes' said the sublime Master, 'I will explain the wisdom state to you. Be razor sharp. Keep your tongue relaxed so the tip is resting on the roof of your mouth and your stomach is quiet and [your appetite] restrained. (716)

39 Let go of the chained minds, the states involving attachment. Do not spend much time thinking about irrelevancies. No defilements, no ties, no dependency: only dedication to the practices of a pure life. (717)

40 In the discipline of living alone, in the service of hermits, it is the silence of solitude that is wisdom. When the solitude becomes a source of pleasure, (718)

41 Then it shines in all the ten directions. This is the sound of the meditation of wisdom, of those who have let sense pleasures go. When you, a follower, hear this sound then you grow in confidence, modesty and strength of practice. (719)

42 Listen to the sound of water. Listen to the water running through chasms and rocks. It is the minor streams that make a loud noise; the great waters flow silently. (720)

43 The hollow resounds and the full is still. Foolishness is like a half-filled pot; the wise man is a lake full of water. (721)

44 The hermit can talk of many things with good sense and precision. He can describe the Way Things Are from a position of knowledge. There is much that he can talk about from that position. (722)

45 But when a man of knowledge retains his self-control, when a man of knowledge speaks only a little, then you have found a man of wisdom, a man for whom that silence is appropriate and deserved. Such a man has found the Silence of Wisdom'. (723)

Note

1 See note 3 to the Ratana Sutta (above).

12. DVAYATĀNUPASSANĀ SUTTA

Origination and Cessation (of suffering)

Thus have I heard: Once the Buddha was staying in the Eastern Park of Migāramātu's estate at Sāvatthi. One evening on a full-moon day he was sitting in the open air with all the monks gathered round him. He saw that they were silent and so he spoke to them.

'Monks', he said, 'It sometimes happens in this world that things are said concerning skilful states, distinguished and liberating statements are made that lead to full enlightenment.

Now, monks, why should you bother to listen to those statements? People may ask you this same question, and, if they do, you should answer them like this:

"It is for the purpose of knowing two things as they have come to be."

They may ask you what these two ideas are, if they do, you should answer them like this:

'The first insight is this: this is suffering and this is what causes it. The second insight is this: that is where suffering stops, and that is how you get there."

These are the twofold insights; grasp them together and, in the course of a life of energy, dedication and care, you can expect one of two results; there will either be the fruit of perfect knowledge, or, if any essential components are not yet exhausted, there will at least be no further births.'

When the Buddha had said this to the monks, he went on, as Teacher, to explain:

1 There are people who do not understand suffering. They do not know where it comes from, where it totally ends, or how to get to where it ends. (724)

2 So, without a chance to emancipate the mind or achieve emancipation through knowledge, they cannot effect an ending; they can only go on and on, being born and getting old. (725)

3 There are also people who comprehend suffering, who know how it happens, where it totally ends and how to get to where it ends. (726)

4 They have got the emancipation of mind and the emancipation through knowledge: now they can effect an ending: no more going on and on, being born and getting old. (727)

This is the proper twofold insight, but you may be asked to describe it in another way and that you could do like this:

'One insight is that grasping is the basis of all suffering. The other insight is that by the complete cooling and cessation of all this grasping there is no more arising of suffering.'

These are the two insights; grasp them together and, with energy, dedication and care, you can expect one of those two results.

5 There are many kinds of suffering in this world and all of them grow from the same source — grasping. When a man knows no better he gives way to this grasping and, slowed and dulled, he goes through one misery after another. So do not create it for yourselves — use your knowledge to see how suffering begins and develops in attachment. (728)

There is another way of describing this twofold insight:

'One insight is that ignorance is the basis of all suffering. The other is that by the complete cooling and cessation of ignorance no more suffering is produced.'

These are the two insights; grasp them together and, with energy, dedication and care, you can expect one of those two results.

6 Constant travelling from birth to birth, from this form to that form, again and again — this is what results from ignorance. (729)

7 It is due to this ignorance that people ['s minds] become dulled and muddled, that they go on endlessly wandering from life to life. But if you walk towards knowledge, you leave these rebirths behind, you do not go on becoming. (730)

There is another way of describing this twofold insight:

'One insight is that: impulses are the basis of all forms of suffering. The other is that by the complete cooling and cessation of impulses no more suffering is produced.'

These are the two insights; grasp them together and, with energy, dedication and care, you can expect one of those two results.

8 Every form of suffering grows out of a mental impulse. Eradicate the impulses and no more suffering is produced. (731)

9 Consider this harmful consequence of the impulses, that they are the basis of suffering. By the complete calming of the impulses and the stopping of the train of perceptions, suffering disappears. (732)

10 Wise men understand this in accordance with fact. With right knowledge the wise ones overcome the yoke of Māra. There is no more rebirth for them. (733)

There is another way of describing this twofold insight:

'One insight is that consciousness is the basis of all suffering. The other is that by the complete cooling and cessation of consciousness no more suffering is produced.'

These are the two insights; grasp them together and, with energy, dedication and care, you can expect one of those two results.

11 Every form of suffering grows out of consciousness. By the cessation of consciousness no more suffering is produced. (734)

12 Consider this harmful consequence of consciousness, that it is the basis of suffering. But once consciousness is quietened, a person's craving ends: total calm is realized. (735)

There is another way of describing this twofold insight:

'One insight is that contact is the basis of suffering. The other is that by the complete cooling and cessation of contact no more suffering is produced.'

These are the two insights: grasp them together and, with energy, dedication and care, you can expect one of those two results.

13 For some people, contact, the point where sense plus object meet, is enthralling. And so they are washed by the tides of being, drifting along an empty, pointless road. Nowhere is there any sign of broken chains. (736)

14 But others come to understand their sense activity and because they understand it, the stillness fills them with delight. They see just what contact does, and so their craving ends; they realize the total calm. (737)

There is another way of describing this twofold insight:

'One insight is that sensations are the basis of all suffering. The other is that by the complete cooling and cessation of sensation no more suffering is produced.'

These are the two insights; grasp them together and, with energy, dedication and care, you can expect one of those two results.

15 – 16 Whether it is pleasurable sensation or unpleasant sensation or neutral sensation, whatever is sensed internally or externally one should understand all this as suffering, as deluding experience, as fragile experience; one should see with insight its rising and falling nature and by this means should be detached towards it. The monk becomes free from craving and completely calmed by the elimination of sensations. (738 – 9)

There is another way of describing this twofold insight:

'One insight is that the thirst of craving is the basis of suffering. The other is that by the complete cooling and cessation of this thirst no more suffering is produced.'

These are the two insights; grasp them together and, with energy, dedication and care, you can expect one of those two results.

17 When a man walks hand in hand with the thirst of craving, he will wander from birth to birth, now here, now there, and with never an end in sight. (740)

18 Consider this harmful consequence of craving, that it is the basis of suffering, and with this knowledge you could let the thirst dissolve. The clinging would go with it and you would be free to live, always mindful, as a wanderer. (741)

There is another way of describing this twofold insight:

'One insight is that clinging is the basis of all suffering. The other is that by the complete cooling and cessation of clinging no more suffering is produced.'

These are the two insights; grasp them together and, with energy, dedication and care, you can expect one of those two results.

19 Becoming is dependent on clinging. When one becomes one comes to suffering. A person who is born dies also. This is the production of suffering. (742)

20 And so, perfected in understanding, the wise dissipate all clinging. They have seen how the forces of becoming can be stopped. So they do not go towards more births. (743)

There is another way of describing this twofold insight:

'One insight is that effort is the basis of all suffering. The other insight is that by the complete cooling and cessation of effort no more suffering is produced.'

These are the two insights; grasp them together and, with energy, dedication and care, you can expect one of those two results.

21 Every form of suffering grows out of effort. Eradicate effort and no more suffering is produced. (744)

22 Consider this evil consequence of effort, that it is the basis of suffering. But when all effort has been abandoned, there is the freedom of the effortless. (745)

23 For the person whose feverish thirst to be is destroyed, and the mind has become calm, the cycle of birth and rebirth is left behind and there is no more coming back for rebirth. (746)

There is another way of describing this twofold insight:

'One insight is that nutrients are the basis of all suffering. The other is that by the complete cooling and cessation of nutrients no more suffering is produced.'

These are the two insights; grasp them together and, with energy, dedication and care, you can expect one of those two results.

24 Every form of suffering grows out of nutrients. Eradicate these nutrients and no more suffering is produced. (747)

25 Look at the harmful consequences of nutrients, that they are the basis of suffering. When you have comprehended all nutrients you do not get attached to them. (748)

26 When someone fully understands what is healthy then he can do away with the mental poisons. He can stand firm and clear-sighted in the practice of the Teachings, as a person fulfilled, as a being beyond definition. (749)

There is another way of describing this twofold insight:

'One insight is that mental agitations are the basis of all suffering. The other is that by the complete cooling and cessation of these agitations no more suffering is produced.'

These are the two insights; grasp them together and, with energy, dedication and care, you can expect one of those two results.

27 Every form of suffering grows out of agitation. Eradicate agitation and no more suffering is produced. (750)

28 Consider this harmful consequence of agitations, that they are productive of misery. Therefore, give up agitation, break the impulses and free from agitation and clinging, let the monk mindfully wander along. (751)

There is another way of describing this twofold insight:

'One insight is that there is trembling for one who is dependent. The other is that the one independent does not tremble.'

These are the two insights; grasp them together and, with effort, dedication and care, you can expect one of those two results.

29 The independent man does not tremble or get confused. But a man who is dependent on something is clutching, grasping at existence in one form or another, and he cannot escape from existences. (752)

30 Consider this evil consequence, that there is grave danger in being dependent. Therefore, relying on nothing, the mindful monk wanders on, free from clinging. (753)

There is another way of describing this twofold insight:

'One insight is that there is more calm in the formless than in the formed. The other is that there is more calm in cessation than in the formless'.

These are the two points; grasp them together and, with effort, dedication and care, you can expect one of those two results.

31 Beings who do not understand cessation will come back to the process of rebecoming, whether those beings be those of the sphere of form or of the sphere of the formless. (754)

32 But those beings who, having understood the nature of form, are well established in the formless and free themselves in cessation are the ones who leave death behind them. (755)

There is another way of describing this twofold insight:

'One insight is that what the world at large, inclusive of its māras, recluses, brahmins, as well as men and rulers, thinks of as truth, the higher beings, the men of worth, see quite clearly, through their superior wisdom, as false. The other is that what the world at large, . . . thinks of as false, the higher beings, the men of worth, see quite clearly as the truth.'

These are the two insights; grasp them together and, with energy, dedication and care, you can expect one of those two results.

33 In the world, inclusive of its gods, substance is seen in what is insubstantial. They are tied to their psychophysical beings and so they think that there is some substance, some reality in them. (756)

34 But whatever be the phenomenon through which they think of seeking their self identity, it turns out to be transitory. It becomes false, for what lasts for a moment is deceptive. (757)

35 The state that is not deceptive is Nibbāna: that is what the men of worth know as being real. With this insight into reality their hunger ends: cessation, total calm. (758)

There is another way of describing this twofold insight:

'One insight is that what the world at large, . . . thinks of as pleasure, the higher beings see quite clearly is suffering. The other is that what the world at large, . . . thinks of as suffering, the higher beings see quite clearly with their superior wisdom as blissful.'

These are the two points; grasp them together and, with energy, dedication and care, you can expect one of those two results.

36 Whatever there is which is said to be existent, the delightful, enticing and pleasant forms, sounds, tastes, odours, tactile sensations and thoughts, these are all agreed upon by the world, inclusive of its gods, to be happiness. (759)

37 In your world these things are thought of as pleasures, and yet, when they cease, they are thought of as sufferings. (760)

38 To the higher beings when the individual body and personality comes to an end it is considered to be blissful. But this varies sharply from the way it is seen by the rest of the common world. (761)

39 What is generally called blissful is called suffering by men of worth. And what is generally called suffering is known to be blissful by them. (762)

Be aware of this paradox: it is difficult to understand and the ignorant are in error in this regard.

40 It is dark where they are trapped; it is pitch dark for the blind and crystal clear for the wholesome; for those that can see it there is light.

But if you are blind to the Teachings of the Way Things Are, if you know nothing of the path, then you will not be able to make out anything though you may be right on top of it. (763)

41 This Teaching about the Way Things Are does not become a force of full enlightenment for someone who is infected with desire, yearning to be, or for someome who is in the grip of Māra. (764)

42 For who else can justifiably reach this state of full understanding except for those beings of distinction? Who else has come to understand this state and dispersed all the forces of confusion?' (765)

This is what the Buddha said on that occasion. The monks were full of gladness and joy when they heard these things. Indeed, some sixty monks let go of all clinging and grasping during this talk and they were freed.

IV. The Chapter of the Eights

1. KĀMA SUTTA

Sensual pleasure — to be avoided

1 If he who desires sensual pleasures is successful, he will certainly be gratified, having obtained what a mortal wishes for. (766)

2 But if those sensual pleasures are denied to the person who desires and wishes for them, he will suffer as one pierced with darts. (767)

3 He who avoids sensual pleasures as he would avoid crushing the head of a snake with his foot, such a one, being thoughtful, will conquer this desire. (768)

4–5 He who desires different sense objects, such as estates, gardens, gold, money, horses, servants, relations; passions will overpower him, dangers will crush him and pain will follow him as water leaks into a wrecked ship. (769–70)

6 Therefore, let one always be thoughtful and avoid sensual pleasures; having abandoned them let him cross the flood [of defilements] and, like baling out a damaged ship, go to the further shore [Nibbāna]. (771)

2. GUHAṬṬAKA SUTTA

The Cave

1 That man who is greatly attached to the cave of the body and sunk in delusion, such a one is far from detachment.[1] Sensual pleasures are not easy to abandon in the world. (772)

2 Those who are bound to worldly pleasures, conditioned by craving, are difficult to liberate; they cannot be liberated by others. Perceiving their past and future indulgence they hanker after sensuality. (773)

3 Those who are greedy, engage in and are infatuated by sensual pleasures; who remain stingy in a miserable state, wail: 'What will happen to us after death?' (774)

4 Therefore a person should train himself in the immediate present. If he knows that the world is wicked, he should not take the wicked way. Life is short, say the wise. (775)

5 I observe these trembling beings of the world given to desire for various states of becoming; they are wrecked who cringe at death, not being free from craving for repeated birth. (776)

6 Look at those who struggle after their petty ambitions, like fish in a stream that is fast drying up. Seeing this, let one fare unselfish in this life, while ceasing to worry about various states of becoming. (777)

7 Overcoming desire alike for sensory enjoyment and their causes, comprehending sense impressions, not hankering after enjoyments and not doing what is against one's conscience, the wise one does not get attached to what he sees or hears. (778)

8 Having realized the [nature of] ideas, the sage is not attached to worldly objects. Having pulled out the dart of passion and faring heedfully, he does not crave for this world or the next. (779)

Note

1 Detachment is threefold, viz. (i) bodily detachment (*kāyaviveka*), (ii) mental detachment (*cittaviveka*) and (iii) psycho-ethical detachment (*upadhiviveka*). Niddesa I. 26f.

3. DUṬṬHAṬṬHAKA SUTTA

Corruption

1 Some people speak with malicious intentions and others with the conviction that they are right. But the sage does not enter into any controversy that has arisen. Therefore, the sage is free from all mental obstruction. (780)

2 The person who is led by his impelling desire and continues according to his inclination, finds it difficult to give up those views he adheres to. Coming to conclusions of his own, he speaks in accordance with his knowledge. (781)

3 If a person, without being asked, praises his own virtue and practices to others, or talks of himself, the good say he is ignoble. (782)

4 The calm, disciplined one who abstains from praising himself for his virtues, declaring, 'So I am', the good call him a noble. In him there is no arrogance concerning the world. (783)

5 He whose views are mentally constructed, causally formed, highly esteemed but not pure; views in which he sees personal advantage, will experience a calm which is unstable. (784)

6 It is hard to go beyond preconceived ideas reached by passing judgment regarding doctrines. Therefore, with regard to these views he rejects one and grasps another. (785)

7 For the person with spiritual excellence, nowhere in the world does he have any mentally-constructed view about various spheres of becoming. As he has eradicated delusion and deceit, in what manner can he be reckoned? He cannot be reckoned in any manner whatsoever. (786)

8 He who is attached enters into debate about doctrines. By what and how can an unattached person be characterized? He has nothing to grasp or reject; he has purified all views here itself. (787)

4. SUDDHAṬṬHAKA SUTTA

Purity

1 'I see a pure, noble and healthy man; a person's purification emerges from what he sees' — thus, holding this opinion and having seen this view to be the best, he considers knowledge to consist in the seeing of a pure being. (788)

2 If a man's purity comes from what is seen, or if by this knowledge he can be freed of sorrow, then something other than the Noble Path makes the person grasping after things a pure one. This view itself reveals the nature of this person. (789)

3 No brahmin claims purity from an external source such as what is seen, heard, or cognized, or from rule or rite. Unsullied by both merit and demerit he has discarded the ego; he does not commit here any action productive of [rebecoming] results. (790)

4 Those who leave one thing to take up another and follow attachment never relinquish desire. They are like monkeys who let go of one branch to grasp another, only to let it go again. (791)

5 The man who, having undertaken certain holy practices himself, attached to ideas, passes from superior to inferior states. But the wise man, having understood the Truth by the [supreme] means of knowledge does not pass from superior to inferior states. (792)

6 He who has dissociated himself from whatever is seen, heard or cognized. How can one have doubts about such an insightful person who conducts himself openly? (793)

7 They do not speculate, they do not esteem any views and say 'This is the highest purity'. They release the knot of dogmatic clinging and do not long for anything in the world. (794)

8 The brahmin who has transcended the limits of mundane existence; he has no grasping after knowing or seeing. He delights neither in passion nor in dispassion. For him there is nothing here to be grasped as the highest. (795)

5. PARAMAṬṬHAKA SUTTA

Perfection

1 The person abiding by a certain dogmatic view, considering it is the highest in the world, claims 'This is the most excellent', and disparages other views different from that as inferior. As a result, he is not free from disputes. (796)

2 When he sees personal advantages from the things that he has seen, heard or cognized, or from rule or rite, he clings passionately to that alone and sees everything else as inferior. (797)

3 The experts say that it is a bond to depend on what one associates with and to see everything else as inferior. Therefore, the disciplined one should not trust in things seen, heard or felt or in rules and rites. (798)

4 A disciplined man does not engender dogmatic views in the world either by knowledge or by rule or rite. Therefore, he does not consider himself 'superior', 'inferior' or 'equal'. (799)

5 The sage has abandoned the notion of self or ego and is free from clinging. He does not depend even on knowledge; he does not take sides in the midst of controversy; he has no dogmatic views. (800)

6 For him there is no desire to strive for this or that, in this world or the next. He has ceased to associate with dogmas for he no longer requires the solace that dogmas offer. (801)

7 To the sage there is not the slightest prejudiced view with regard to things seen, heard or felt. How can anyone in the world characterize by thought such a pure one who does not dogmatically grasp any views? (802)

8 They neither form any particular dogma nor prefer anything. Dogmatic views are not esteemed by them. The brahmin is not led by rule and rite. Thus, the steadfast one has gone to the further shore, never more to return. (803)

6. JARĀ SUTTA

Decay

1 Short indeed is this life; one dies within a hundred years, but if anyone survives longer than that he surely dies of decay. (804)

2 People grieve for the things they are attached to as 'mine', but there is no enduring object of grasping. Comprehending this situation, the wise one should lead a homeless life. (805)

3 What one grasps thinking, 'this is mine', is left behind by death. Recognizing this fact, let not the wise one who follows the right path turn to acquisitiveness. (806)

4 The awakened man does not see what he has dreamt in sleep; likewise one does not see the beloved that has passed away and is dead. (807)

5 Seen and heard are those people whose particular names are mentioned; but only the name of a person remains when he has passed away. (808)

6 The selfish, greedy ones do not give up sorrow, lamentation and miserliness. Hence, the sages, giving up objects of grasping, wander about with insight into tranquillity. (809)

7 For the disciplined one who leads a contemplative life and cultivates a mind of seclusion, it is to be expected that he will not continue in existence. (810)

8 The sage who is independent in all circumstances, does not exhibit like or dislike. Sorrow and avarice do not cling to him as water does not stick to the lotus leaf. (811)

9 As a drop of water does not stick to a lotus leaf or as a lotus flower is untainted by the water, so the sage does not cling to anything — seen, heard or thought. (812)

10 The liberated one does not seek anything that is seen, heard or thought. He does not seek purity through anything else for he has neither passion nor dispassion. (813)

7. TISSAMETTEYYA SUTTA

Tissametteyya

In praise of celibacy

Tissametteyya:
1 Tell me, O gracious Sir, the mishaps for him who is given to sexual intercourse. By learning your admonition we will train ourselves in seclusion. (814)

The Buddha:
2 Both learning and the practice of the Teaching are lost to him who is given to sexual intercourse. He employs himself wrongly. That is what is ignoble in him. (815)

3 He who formerly fared alone but is now given to sexual intercourse, they call that uncontrolled one a low and ordinary being who is like a lurching chariot. (816)

4 What fame and renown he had before is lost to him. Having seen this, he should train to give up sexual intercourse. (817)

5 He who is overcome by thoughts, broods thereon like a miserable fellow and, having heard the reproach of others, he becomes depressed. (818)

6 Tormented by the words of others, he injures his life by wrongdoing. He becomes attached and plunges into falsehood. (819)

7 First they thought him 'a wise one' when he took up the solitary life, but since he has given himself up to sexual intercourse, they call him 'a fool'. (820)

8 Realizing this danger in the world from beginning to the end, the sage keeps strictly to his solitary life. He does not give himself up to sexual intercourse. (821)

9 Let him train in the solitary life, for that is the noble life. Because of that he should not think himself the best. He, truly, is the person who is at the threshold of liberation [Nibbāna]. (822)

10 The tranquil and solitary sage remains free from sensual desires and has crossed the stream of such tendencies. He is indeed envied by those attached to carnal bonds. (823)

8. PASŪRA SUTTA

Disputation — and its futility

1 They say that purity is theirs alone; they do not say that there is purity in the teachings of others. Whatever teaching they have devoted themselves to, they claim that as the most excellent and thus separately hold diverse truths. (824)

2 The debaters, having entered into the gathering, start disputes calling each other fools; since they are depending on certain teachers, they seek praise, calling themselves the experts. (825)

3 Engaged in disputations in the midst of a gathering, one becomes frustrated in one's quest for praise. In defeat he becomes downcast and, seeking for flaws in others, becomes enraged by their criticism. (826)

4 When those who have tested his questions say that his talk is faulty, he laments, grieves and wails in his worthless disputes saying, 'They have defeated me!' (827)

5 These disputes arise among recluses and as a result of them there is elation and depression. Seeing this, avoid disputation. There is no value in it other than the praise won thereby. (828)

6 He who is praised in the midst of a gathering for having successfully defended his view, will be thrilled with joy and be much elated in mind for having won his case. (829)

7 Elation itself is the ground of his downfall; for still he talks with pride and arrogance. Seeing this, one should not dispute; for the wise never say that purification is achieved thereby. (830)

8 Like the bold one nourished by good food, he goes forth roaring looking for a rival. Wherever there is such a rival you may go there. But here, there is nothing left as before which could provoke a fight. (831)

9 Those who have embraced a certain theory and argue over it maintaining that that alone is the truth, you may talk with such people. But here, 'there is no opponent to battle with you'. (832)

10 Those who fare on, having overcome opposition without countering any one theory with another, what would you obtain, O bold one, from them? For them there is nothing embraced as the highest. (833)

11 Speculating in your mind on different philosophical views, you have come reflecting on them. But you cannot go along yoked together with the one who is purified. (834)

9. MĀGANDIYA SUTTA

Māgandiya

(*Similar to the preceding Sutta*)

(The dialogue between Māgandiya and the Buddha on the occasion of the former's offer of his daughter as a wife to the Buddha.)

1 The Buddha: 'Even seeing (Māra's daughters[1]) — Taṇhā (craving) Rati (attachment) and Ragā (passion) — there was not the least arising of carnal desire in me for intercourse. What is this thing full of urine and excrement? I would not like even to touch it with my foot! (835)

2 Māgandiya: If you do not want such a jewel, a maiden desired by many kings, tell me what is your view, what is your way of life in accordance with virtue and practice, and your future destiny. (836)

3 The Buddha: O Māgandiya, after studying what men hold fast to, I do not say 'This I declare'. Seeing all these views, but not grasping them and searching for the truth, I found inward peace. (837)

4 Māgandiya: Noble sage, without grasping those judgments incorporated in the speculative systems, you talk of inward peace. How is it described by the wise? (838)

5 The Buddha: I do not say one attains 'purification' by view, tradition, knowledge, virtue or ritual, nor is it attained without view, tradition, knowledge, virtue or ritual. It is only taking these factors as the means and not grasping them as ends in themselves that one so attains and consequently does not crave for rebecoming. (839)

6 Māgandiya: If you do not say that 'purification' is not attained by view, tradition, knowledge and ritual nor by absence of these — it seems to me that your lore is a nonsense, because some deem 'purification' is from view. (840)

7 The Buddha: Because of your view you are continually asking these questions. It is because you are obsessed with your preconceived notions that you are holding fast. From this you have not perceived the least sense: that is why you see this as nonsense. (841)

8 He who thinks himself 'equal', 'inferior' or 'superior' to others, by that very reason enters disputation. But there are not such thoughts 'equal', 'inferior' or 'superior' to him who is unmoved by these three measurements. (842)

9 Why should the arahant argue with whom he contends saying 'This is a truth' or 'That is a lie'? If one has no such thoughts 'equal' or 'unequal', with whom should he enter into dispute? (843)

10 The sage who has forsaken his home, not entering upon intimate relations in villages, free from lust, not giving preference [to mundane desire] — he does not engage in disputatious talk with people. (844)

11 The noble one who wanders in the world, liberated from views, does not grasp them and enter into arguments. As the thorny lotus rises on its stalk unsoiled by mud and water, so the sage, speaker of peace and free from desire, is unsoiled by the world and its carnal pleasures. (845)

12 That wise one does not become conceited through views or knowledge, for he is not attached to that sort. He is neither enticed by action nor by learning, being detached in every circumstance. (846)

13 There are no ties to him who is free from ideas, there are no delusions to him who is delivered by wisdom. Those who grasp ideas and views, wander about coming into conflict in the world. (847)

Note

1 Synonymous with tempting thoughts.

10. PURĀBHEDA SUTTA

Qualities of a Muni

1 'Gotama, sir,' a questioner said to the Buddha, 'I want to ask you about the perfect man. There are those people whom we call "men who are calmed" — can you tell me how they see things and how they behave?' (848)

2 'A man who is calmed, who has extinguished all his cravings before the time his body disintegrates into nothing, who has no concern with how things began or with how they will end and no fixation with what happens in between: such a man has no preferences. (849)

3 He has no anger, no fear and no pride. Nothing disturbs his composure and nothing gives him cause for regret. He is the wise man who is restrained in speech. (850)

4 He has no longing for the future and no grief for the past; there are no views or opinions that lead him. He can see detachment from the entangled world of sense-impression. (851)

5 He does not conceal anything and there is nothing he holds on to. Without acquisitiveness or envy, he remains unobtrusive; he has no disdain or insult for anyone. (852)

6 He is not a man who is full of himself, or a man who is addicted to pleasure; he is a man who is gentle and alert, with no blind faith; he shows no aversion [to anything]. (853)

7 He is not a person who works because he wants something; if he gets nothing at all he remains unperturbed. There is no craving to build up the passion to taste new pleasures. (854)

8 His mindfulness holds him posed in a constant even-mindedness where arrogance is impossible; he makes no comparisons with the rest of the world as "superior", "inferior" or "equal". (855)

9 Because he understands the Way Things Are, he is free from dependency and there is nothing he relies on. For him there is no more craving to exist or not to exist. (856)

10 This is what I call a man who is calmed. It is a man who does not seek after pleasure, who has nothing to tie him down, who has gone beyond the pull of attachment. (857)

11 It is a man without sons, a man without wealth, without fields, without cows — a man with nothing in him that he grasps at as his and nothing in him that he rejects as not his. (858)

12 He is a man who receives false criticisms from other people, from priests and hermits but who remains undisturbed and unmoved by their words. (859)

13 It is a man without greed and without possessiveness; it is a man who, as a man of wisdom, does not consider himself "superior", "inferior" or "equal". It is a man who does not enter speculation a man who is free from speculations. (860)

14 It is a man who has nothing in this world that he calls his own and who does not grieve for not having anything. He is calmed who does not take speculative views.' (861)

11. KALAHAVIVĀDA SUTTA

Disputes and Contention

(*The causes of anger and attachment*)

1 'Sir', said a questioner, 'whenever there are arguments and quarrels there are tears and anguish, arrogance and pride and grudges and insults to go with them. Can you explain how these things come about? Where do they all come from?' (862)

2 'The tears and anguish that follow arguments and quarrels', said the Buddha, 'the arrogance and pride and the grudges and insults that go with them are all the result of one thing. They come from having preferences, from holding things precious and dear. Insults are born out of arguments and grudges are inseparable from quarrels.' (863)

3 'But why, Sir, do we have these preferences, these special things? Why do we have so much greed? And all the aspirations and achievements that we base our lives on, where do we get them from?' (864)

4 'The preferences, the precious things', said the Buddha, 'come from the impulse of desire. So too does the greed and so too do the aspirations and achievements that make up people's lives'. (865)

5 'From where, Sir, comes this impulse of desire? From where do we derive our theories and opinions? And what about all the other things that you, the Wanderer, have named — such as anger, dishonesty and confusion?' (866)

6 'The impulse of desire arises when people think of one thing as pleasant and another as unpleasant: that is the source of desire. It is when people see that material things are subject both to becoming and to disintegration that they form their theories about the world. (867)

7 Anger, confusion and dishonesty arise when things are set in pairs as opposites. The person with perplexity must train himself in the path of knowledge. The recluse has declared the Truth after realization.' (868)

8 'But why, Sir, is it that we find some things pleasant and some unpleasant? What could we do to stop that? And this idea of becoming and disintegration, could you explain where that comes from?' (869)

9 'It is the action of contact, of mental impression, that leads to the feelings of pleasant and unpleasant. Without the contact they would not exist. And, as I see it, the idea of becoming and disintegration also comes from this source, from the action of contact.' (870)

10 'So what, Sir, does this contact come from? And the grasping habit, what's the reason for that? Is there anything that can be done to get rid of possessiveness and anything that could be eliminated so that there would be no more contact?' (871)

11 'Contact exists because the compound of mind and matter exists. The habit of grasping is based on wanting things. If there were no wanting, there would be no possessiveness. Similarly, without the element of form, of matter, there would be no contact.' (872)

12 'What pursuit leads a person to get rid of form? And how can suffering and pleasure cease to exist? This is what I want to know about.' (873)

13 'There is a state where form ceases to exist', said the Buddha. 'It is a state without ordinary perception and without disordered perception and without no perception and without any annihilation of perception. It is perception, consciousness, that is the source of all the basic obstacles.' (874)

14 'Sir, you have explained to us everything we have asked you about. There is one more question we would like you to answer for us: Do the learned scholars of the world say that this is the highest purification of the individual being or do they say that there is some other kind of goal?' (875)

15 'There are scholars and authorities', replied the Buddha, 'who say that this is the highest and the purification of the individual. There are others who maintain that the highest purity is to be found in the complete eradication of the five components of the person. (876)

16 And there is also the muni, the wise man. He has realized which things are dependencies and he knows that these are only crutches and props. And when he has realized this, he has become free. He does not enter into arguments and so does not enter the round of endless becomings.' (877)

12. CŪLAVIYŪHA SUTTA

Minor Causes of Contention

1 Questioner: Some who abide strictly to their own views alone, come into dispute with others, each claiming that they themselves are the only experts, declaring thus: 'One who understands this, knows the Truth; whoever rejects this is imperfect.' (878)

2 So, having thus got into arguments, they dispute (amongst themselves). They say 'the other person is a fool not an expert'. Since one and all are expert talkers, which is the true statement out of these? (879)

3 The Buddha: If one who does not tolerate another's view is a fool, a dolt and stupid, then all of them are fools without understanding, because all of them abide by their [own] views only. (880)

4 If by reason of one's view one becomes pure, pure in wisdom, expert and intelligent — then there is none among them who is of inferior wisdom, for they have all equally arrived at [dogmatic] views. (881)

5 I do not say that whatever the fools separately advocate is true. They make their own individual views true. Therefore, they determine that another person is a fool. (882)

6 Questioner: What some say is true and real, others say is empty and false. Thus they come to conflict and debate. Why do the recluses not propound one doctrine? (883)

7 The Buddha: The truth is indeed one and the knower of it does not dispute it. There is not a second [view]. Because diverse truths are proclaimed, the ascetics do not say one and the same. (884)

8 Questioner: Why do the disputants who assert themselves to be the experts proclaim 'truths' so diverse? Are there in reality diverse truths or are they following their own reasoning? (885)

9 The Buddha: There are not many diverse truths in the world except those which are surmised by [faulty] perception. Assuming mere sophistry in their views, they claim a duality — 'This is true and that is false.' (886)

10 The fool depends on what is seen, heard or cognized, and rule or rite and looks down upon others saying 'The other person is a fool, an imperfect one', making his own judgment and being happy with it. (887)

11 Just because one who thinks another is a fool and therefore calls himself an expert, such a person who calls himself an expert insults himself and others. (888)

12 The one who is full of rigid, fixed views, puffed up with pride and arrogance, who deems himself 'perfect', becomes annointed in his own opinion because he holds firmly to his own view. (889)

13 If one becomes low by another's word, one becomes one of low wisdom along with the other. And if on one's own one becomes learned and wise then there is none among recluses who is a fool. (890)

14 'Those who proclaim a doctrinal view different from this have misunderstood.' Thus the heretics proclaim many diverse views because they are attached to their own views. (891)

15 Those who are attached to their [own] views maintain that purity [of view] is with them and they deny purity [of view] in other doctrines. Thus these heretics are deeply attached to their own views. (892)

16 The heretic who maintains firmly that his own view is right, who else would he brand a fool? He who calls others 'fool' and 'holder of impure doctrine' would indeed invite strife. (893)

17 Standing rigidly to his own view and depending on his own criteria, he enters into dispute in the world. Desisting from all theories the wise one does not enter into dispute in the world. (894)

13. MAHĀVIYŪHA SUTTA

Major Causes of Contention

1 Those who, adhering to their views, dispute 'this only is the truth', either bring blame upon themselves or obtain praise thereby. (895)

2 The result of the praise is trifling and not enough to bring about tranquillity. I say there are two results of dispute [victory or defeat]; having seen this, let no one dispute, realizing Nibbāna where there is no dispute. (896)

3 The wise one does not embrace all those views that have arisen amongst worldly people. Should he who is free from views be pleased with what has been seen and heard and remain dependent on them? (897)

4 Those who consider moral practices to be the highest say: 'purity comes through restraint; having undertaken a holy practice, let us train in it whence purity comes.' But those so-called experts are still immersed in Saṃsāra. (898)

5 If he falls away from moral conduct and holy practices, he trembles, having failed in his action; he longs here for purity like a traveller who has lost his caravan while he is away from his home. (899)

6 Having abandoned formal religious practices altogether and actions both 'good' and 'bad', neither longing for 'purity' nor 'impurity', he wanders aloof abstaining from both without adhering to either extreme. (900)

7 Practising loathsome penances or adhering to what has been seen, heard or thought, they praise purity in high voices — but they are not free from craving for recurring existence. (901)

8 For him who desires, more desires result; he trembles, deluded by imaginary views. For him who has overcome death and birth why should he tremble and what would he yearn for? (902)

9 What some regard as the highest view others consider to be worthless. They all claim to be experts: which of them indeed is right? (903)

10 Each one claims that his own view is perfect and that the belief of others is inferior. Thus they enter into dispute; thus each of them says that his own opinion is true. (904)

11 If a view becomes worthless because it is censured by others, then no one will be distinguished because each one firmly regards another's view as low whilst one's own alone is regarded as true. (905)

12 Just as they honour their views, likewise they praise their ways. If all their views are true then their purity must also be peculiar to them. (906)

13 To the noble one there is no lead from others, nothing to embrace after investigation of views; he, therefore, has transcended disputation, for he does not see another's view as the best. (907)

14 'I know and see, this is just so' — thus saying, some claim purity through that view. What is the point in saying that one has 'seen' (the truth) if rival views are put forward. (908)

15 The man sees mind and matter and having seen he takes them as permanent. Let him see either much or little for experts do not say: 'purity comes by that'. (909)

16 Not easy to discipline the dogmatist who says this is the truth, being misguided by views. Saying that good is in such preconceptions, he is given to saying that purity is inherent as he has so seen. (910)

17 The noble one having perceived things through knowledge, does not enter into speculations. Having learnt of diverse theories that have arisen among others, he is indifferent to them whilst others labour to embrace them. (911)

18 The sage, being freed from worldly ties, remains peaceful among the restless. He is indifferent among sectarian squabbles, not embracing them whilst others remain attached. (912)

19 Having abandoned former defilements, not inducing new ones, not becoming partisan, he is free from dogmatic views. Being wise, he neither clings to the world nor blames himself. (913)

20 By overcoming all the theories based on seen, heard or thought he is a sage who has released his burden and is liberated, not imaginative in views, not aspiring for anything — so said the Buddha. (914)

14. TUVAṬAKA SUTTA

The Way to Bliss

(*A portrayal of the ideal monk*)

1 'Master of Wisdom, descendant of the Sun', said a questioner to the Buddha, 'I wish to question you about the state of peace, the state of solitude and quiet detachment. With what manner of insight does a monk become calm, cooled and no longer grasps at anything?' (915)

2 'He achieves this', replied the Master, 'by cutting out the root obstacle, the delusion: he eradicates all thought of "I am ". By being mindful all the time he trains himself to let go of all the cravings that arise in him. (916)

3 Whatever he may understand inwardly or outwardly, he has to avoid becoming proud of his convictions. For good men have said that this is not the state of calm. (917)

4 He has to avoid thinking of himself as better or worse than, or equal to anyone. Coming into contact with various things, he should not embellish the self. (918)

5 The monk must look for peace within himself and not in any other place. For when a person is inwardly quiet, there is nowhere a self can be found; where, then, could a non-self be found? (919)

6 There are no waves in the depths of the sea; it is still, unbroken. It is the same with the monk. He is still, without any quiver of desire, without a remnant on which to build pride and desire.' (920)

7 'Sir', said the questioner, 'you have explained with clear words and with open eyes the way that removes all dangers. Could you please tell me now about the practices of the path, the rules that must be kept and also about the development of concentration?' (921)

8 'The Master replied: 'A monk keeps his eyes from wandering restlessly with desire and his ears are deaf to chatter and gossip. He has no longing for new sweets to taste; nor has he any desire to possess things in the world as his own. (922)

9 Where he is in contact with sense impressions he should not become sorrowful or sad. He should not begin to wish for some other kind of life or tremble when confronted with fearful things. (923)

10 When he is given rice and other food to eat, or milk to drink, or clothes to wear, then, as a monk, he should not begin to store them up. And he should not be anxious if he does not get any of them. (924)

11 He has to become a man of meditation, not a loiterer, and a man without any regrets or laziness. He is a monk, and, sitting or lying down, he spends his time in his quiet living-place. (925)

12 He should not sleep too much and he should make constant effort to be watchful whilst he is awake. Laziness, deception, laughter, games, sexual intercourse, ornaments: all these he has to give up. (926)

13 He does not study the practice of magic and spells. He does not analyse dreams and signs in sleep and movements in the Zodiac. As one of my followers, he should not spend time interpreting bird-songs or curing infertility or selling medicines and cures. (927)

14 The monk should not be perturbed by criticism or impressed by praise. There is no place for greed in him; hoarding, anger and slander are emotions he has to discard. (928)

15 He should not get involved in buying and selling, and he should learn not to blame anything on other people. When he meets people in the village he must not speak to them in the hope of getting some reward. (929)

16 He should not boast, should not speak carelessly, should not train himself in impudence or utter quarrelsome talk. (930)

17 The monk should not speak falsehood. He should not wilfully commit dishonest deeds. He should not look down upon another, feeling proud of his livelihood, wisdom or observance of rule and rite. (931)

18 And when he hears other wanderers and ordinary people using angry words, he does not retort with harsh speech; for men of goodness do not answer back. (932)

19 Understanding this norm, the inquiring monk should train himself being constantly mindful. When the realization comes that peace can be found in the state of calm, then he should apply himself completely to the teaching of Gotama. (933)

20 He is the undefeated conqueror: he saw with his own eyes the Way Things Are; he did not borrow it from tradition. So, with constant diligence and respect, the monk should apply himself to the teaching of this Master.' (934)

15. ATTADAṆḌA SUTTA

Violent Conduct

(*A portrayal of perfect freedom similar to the preceding Sutta*)

1 Fear results from resorting to violence — just look at how people quarrel and fight! But let me tell you now of the kind of dismay and terror that I have felt. (935)

2 Seeing people struggling, like fish, writhing in shallow water with enmity against one another, I became afraid. (936)

3 At one time, I had wanted to find some place where I could take shelter, but I never saw any such place. There is nothing in this world that is solid at base and not a part of it that is changeless. (937)

4 I had seen them all trapped in mutual conflict and that is why I had felt so repelled. But then I noticed something buried deep in their hearts. It was — I could just make it out — a dart. (938)

5 It is a dart that makes its victims run all over the place. But once it has been pulled out all that running is finished and so is the exhaustion that comes with it. (939)

6 These are the things we can learn from this: The bonds of the world should not be pursued. Disenchanted with all sense pleasures one should train oneself in calmness [Nibbāna]. (940)

7 A man of wisdom should be truthful, without arrogance, without deceit, not slanderous and not hateful. He should go beyond the evil of greed and miserliness. (941)

8 To have your mind set on calmness, you must take power over sleepiness, drowsiness and lethargy. There is no place for laziness and no recourse to pride. (942)

9 Do not be led into lying, do not be attached to forms. You must see through all pride and fare along without violence. (943)

10 Do not get excited by what is old, do not be contented with what is new. Do not grieve for what is lost or be controlled by desire. (944)

11 I call this craving, the greed, a great flood, and the hankering I call attachment, hanging up. This bog of lust is difficult to cross. (945)

12 But the man of wisdom stands on solid ground — he is like a brahmin, never moving from Truth, and when he has completely renounced then indeed is he calm. (946)

13 He has wisdom, he has complete knowledge, he has understood the Way Things Are. He is completely independent. In his perfect wanderings from place to place, he has no envy for anyone. (947)

14 Desire is a chain, shackled to the world, and it is a difficult one to break. But once that is done, there is no more grief and no more longing: the stream has been cut off and there are no more chains. (948)

15 Let there be nothing behind you; leave the future to one side. Do not clutch at what is left in the middle; then you will become a wanderer and calm. (949)

16 When a man does not identify himself with mind and matter at all, when he does not grieve for what does not exist, then he cannot sustain any loss in this world. (950)

17 When he does not think, 'This is mine' or 'That belongs to them', then, since he has no egoism, he cannot grieve with the thought of 'I do not have'. (951)

18 If you ask me to describe a man who is unshakeable, I say that where there is no harshness, where there is no greed, no trace of desire, and when a man is the same in all circumstances, then you have what I would call the praiseworthy condition of a man unshakeable. (952)

19 A man of discernment, without a flutter of desire, does not accumulate — he has no conditioning — he has stopped all effort of every kind; so everywhere he sees peace and happiness. (953)

20 The wise man does not rate himself with the distinguished, the lowest, nor with ordinary people; calm and unselfish, he is free from possessiveness: he holds on to nothing and he rejects nothing. (954)

16. SĀRIPUTTA SUTTA

Sāriputta

The training practice of a monk

Venerable Sāriputta said:
1 Neither have I seen, nor has anyone heard of such a sweet-tongued Master coming down from the Tusita heaven to the midst of the many. (955)

2 The one with vision appears as he really is to the world of men and gods and after having dispelled all darkness he alone attained happiness. (956)

3 Here, from the many, I have come supplicatingly, with a question for the Buddha who is unattached, a guileless teacher who has arrived in the world. (957)

4–5 The monk who abhors the world will seek out a lonely lodging under trees, in mountain caves; to him who delights in these various lodgings what dangers are there? The monk does not tremble in his quiet dwelling. (958–9)

6 How many dangers are there in the world to be overcome by a monk living in solitary dwellings and going towards the region of immortality? (960)

7 What are his words, what are his objects in this world, what are the virtues and practices of the energetic monk? (961)

8 What is the training he has to undertake so that, being concentrated, wise and mindful, he may remove his own impurities as a smith removes the dross from silver? (962)

The Buddha said:
9 O Sāriputta, to you who are disgusted with the world, who delight in a solitary dwelling, and desire perfect enlightenment in accordance with the Truth, I will tell what I have realized. (963)

10 The monk who is wise, mindful and who wanders in the limitations,[1] is not afraid of the five dangers, [viz.] gadflies and all other flies, snakes, men of ill-will or animals. (964)

11 He is not afraid of heretics, even when he has seen the dangers from them. Furthermore, he who is a seeker of good, will overcome other dangers too. (965)

12 He endures cold and excessive heat, even if he is affected by sickness and hunger. Affected by them in many ways, and being homeless, make strong exertions! (966)

13 Let him not steal, let him not speak lies, let him touch with loving-kindness those who are feeble or strong. When he is aware that his mind is agitated let that agitation be driven away by knowing that it belongs to the baser side. (967)

14 Let him not fall under the influence of anger or arrogance; let him stay by having uprooted these and let him overcome both what is pleasant and what is unpleasant. (968)

15 Guided by wisdom, with noble joy, overcoming dangers, let him dispel discontent in his distant solitude. Let him overcome the four lamentations: (969)

16 'What shall I eat, or where shall I eat? I slept [last night] uncomfortably indeed; where shall I sleep tonight?' Let the aspirant who wanders about homeless subdue these lamentable thoughts. (970)

17 Having received in due time both food and robes, he knows moderation in worldly matters for the sake of contentment. Guarded in these things and restrained while wandering in the village, even if he is offended by people he never utters a harsh word. (971)

18 He who walks about with downcast eyes, not loitering, devoted to meditation, should be very watchful. Having acquired equanimity with a composed mind he should cut off base and discursive thoughts and remorse. (972)

19 Let him welcome the words of reproof mindfully. With words of reproach let him break stubbornness in his fellow monks. Let him utter wise words at a proper time. Let him not think detractingly of vulgar people. (973)

20 Then let him mindfully train to discipline the five kinds of pollution in the world, [namely] passion for forms, sounds, tastes, smells and touch. (974)

21 Let the monk who is mindful with well-liberated mind subdue the desire for these things. Then, investigating the Truth thoroughly and with concentration, he will destroy the darkness [of ignorance]. (975)

Note

1 The four limitations (*pariyanta*) are moral self-restraint (*sīlasaṃvara*), restraint of the senses (*indriyasaṃvara*), moderation in food (*bhojanamattaññutā*) and the applications of watchfulness (*jāgiriyānuyoga*).

V. The Chapter of the Way to the Beyond

VATTHUGĀTHĀ

(Prologue)

1 One day a man walked out of the beautiful city of Sāvatthi in Kosala. It was Bāvari the brahmin, one versed in the Vedic mantras. He had set out on the southern road in search of detachment. (976)

2 He travelled till he came to the land of the Assakas and there, where it meets the Aḷaka's land, on the banks of the River Godhāvari, he stayed, living off fruit and whatever else he could gather. (977)

3 One day, begging in a rich village nearby, he was given such a quantity of gifts that he was able to hold a great offering-ceremony. (978)

4 He had just finished the rituals and got back to his hut when another brahmin arrived at the door. (979)

5 He was thirsty, covered with dust, with stains on his teeth and swellings on his feet. He came up to the hermit and begged to be given 500 pence worth of money. (980)

6 As soon as the hermit saw the visitor he made him sit down. After he had asked after his health and happiness he told the man he couldn't help. (981)

7 'You see, brahmin, I've given away everything I've been given. Please forgive me, but I haven't got 500 pence.' (982)

8 'You have rejected the pleading of a beggar!' said the visitor. 'May your head split into seven in seven days' time as a result of this refusal!' (983)

9 And then, before he left, the rascal chanted spells and laid a formal curse on Bāvari, to the brahmin's great distress. (984)

10 In the days that followed the brahmin's pain increased. The sadness and grief were like darts in his side; he couldn't eat, he just wasted away; he couldn't even settle his mind in meditation. (985)

11 But a friendly goddess-spirit saw him in his suffering and fear, and so she came to his hut and talked to him. (986)

12 'He was only an imposter, that man', she said, 'trying to make easy money. Besides he was ignorant — he knows nothing about the head and nothing about head-splitting.' (987)

13 'Goddess', said the brahmin, 'if he doesn't know, then who does? If you understand head-splitting then please tell me all about it. I have to understand it!' (988)

14 'No', said the spirit, 'I can't help you, I don't know a thing about it. The only people who can know about things like that are Conquerors.' (989)

15 'Well then, goddess', said the brahmin, 'you must tell me who in the world I can go to who'll know.' (990)

16 And this is how the goddess replied:
'In the line of the great King Okkaka a boy has been born to the Sākyas. He has gone out of their capital Kapilavatthu; he has gone into the world as a leader and a light. (991)

17 This man, brahmin, has total enlightenment. This man has total perfection. This man has the power of total knowledge, the eye of total vision. He has found the total ending, he has lost the basic grasping and is free. (992)

18 He is enlightenment, he's a Buddha. He's a Lord, a Master of Blessings for the world. He has the eye of vision and he teaches the Way Things Are. Go to him and ask your questions — he will explain it all'. (993)

19 When Bāvari heard that word Sambuddha, the name for total enlightenment, he was lifted to the heights of joy. As his sorrow quietened down, he felt immense delight take him over. (994)

20 The gladness and joy made him eager and deeply thrilled. 'Where', he asked the goddess, 'does this world-guide live? Which village is he in? Which town? Which state? Let's go and honour this man, this ultimate being!' (995)

21 'The Conqueror lives in Sāvatthi in Kosala', said the goddess. 'This Sākyan is a wealth of wisdom and a world of knowledge, he's unharnessed and undefiled, he has the strength of a hero, of a bull. He's the one to ask about head-splitting.' (996)

22 So Bāvari the brahmin called his pupils together, all of them versed in Vedic mantras too. 'Come here, brahmin students', he said, 'and listen to this — I have something to tell you! (997)

23 Something has happened, something that rarely takes place in the world: A Sambuddha has arrived. Yes, a man has been born in the world who is now recognized as fully enlightened! Brahmins, you must go immediately to Sāvatthi to see this perfect being.' (998)

24 'But brahmin Sir', said the students, 'how can we go if we don't know what enlightenment looks like? Tell us, Sir, how to recognize it.' (999)

25 'The Ancient Teachings', said the brahmin, 'listed each one of the thirty-two marks of greatness on a superman. (1000)

26 When a person is born with these marks on his body, then we can say that one of two things will happen to him, that he has two choices open to him, and no more. (1001)

27 He can choose the life of a layman, the home life. Then he will conquer the world, not by force, but by virtue. (1002)

28 Or he can choose to leave his home, to live as a homeless wanderer. And then he will become a Sambuddha, a man-of-worth, a fully-enlightened, incomparable one. (1003)

29 Now, when you think you've found this man you must ask questions in your mind about my age, my family, my body-marks, my rituals and my pupils — and ask about head-splitting too. (1004)

30 If he is the Buddha with perfect penetrating vision, then he will answer aloud the questions you've asked in your minds.' (1005)

31 – 33 As Bāvari talked his brahmin students listened. There were sixteen of them, all of them famous teachers in their own right, namely, Ajita, Tissa-Metteyya, Puṇṇaka, Mettagū, Dhotaka, Upasīva, Nanda, Hemaka, Todeyya, Kappa, Jatukaṇṇī the scholar, Badhrāvudha, Udaya, Posāla, Mogharāja the learned and the great teacher Piṅgiya the wise — all of them were there. (1006 – 8)

34 They were all well known as teachers and as men who found their enjoyment in life through their meditation practice. They were men, it was said, who had not lost the scent of their previous good deeds. (1009)

35 [When Bāvari had finished his instructions to them] they carefully paid their respects and walked past him to his right. With their hide robes and their braided plaits of hair they set off towards the north. (1010)

36 – 38 They travelled through the land of the Aḷakas, coming first to Patiṭṭhāna, then to Mahussati, Ujjeni and Gonaddhā. On they went to Vedisā and Vanasa, to Kosambī and Sāketa, until they came to the greatest of all cities, Sāvatthi. From there they set out again this time for the land of Magadha. They passed on their way through Setavya, Kapilavatthu and the town of

Kusinārā. They went on the Pāvā, to Bhoganāgara [the city of wealth], and then to Vesālī where they came to the beautiful Pāsāṇaka-Cetiya, the Rock Temple. (1011 – 13)

39 They climbed up the mountain path with the zeal and the haste of a merchant drawn to wealth, or a thirsty man to cool water, or a man with sun-stroke to shade. (1014)

40 And there, with the order of monks gathered all around him, sat the Lord, the Blessed One. He was explaining the Dhamma to them: the lion was roaring in the jungle. (1015)

41 Ajita saw the man of full enlightenment. It was like the sun shining without burning, it was like the moon bright and full on a full-moon day. (1016)

42 He could see all the signs of greatness clearly marked on his body. Astonished and overjoyed he stood respectfully to one side and silently thought his first question. (1017)

43 'Tell me', he asked in his mind, 'how old my teacher is. Tell me what his family name is, Tell me how many of the marks of greatness he has got, and how well versed he is in the Vedic mantras. And how many does he teach?' (1018)

44 'He is 120 years old', said the Master aloud. 'His family name is Bāvari. He has three of the body-marks. He has complete knowledge of the three Vedas, (1019)

45 and also of the Commentaries, the Rituals and the Signs. He instructs 500 and he has reached the ultimate stage according to his teaching.' (1020)

46 'Describe Bāvari's body-marks, master-man, desire-cutter', said Ajita silently, 'so that we have no room at all for doubt.' (1021)

47 'These are his three body-marks, young man', said the Master. 'His tongue is large enough to cover his mouth. There is a tuft of hair growing between the eyebrows. And the foreskin completely covers the phallus.' (1022)

48 – 49 Everybody could hear the Master talking to someone they could not see. Who was asking these questions they couldn't hear? Was it some god? they wondered. Was it Indra, Brahmā, or Sakka? Who was the Master talking to? Astonished, they made the folded-hand gesture in respect. (1023 – 24)

50 [Meanwhile Ajita was asking another mental question.] 'Bāvari asked about heads, Master', he thought, 'and about how they're split. Please great teacher, answer this question too.' (1025)

51 'The head', said the Master, 'is Not-Understanding. The head is split in pieces and destroyed by Understanding, with its army of powers in support: confidence, mindfulness, meditation, and determination — energy. These are the powers that split heads.' (1026)

52 With the thrill of exultation stiffening every pore of his body the young brahmin student bared his shoulder from his hide and got down on to the ground at the feet of the Master. (1027)

53 'Sir', he said with this head bowed, 'Lord, Seer, Bāvari the brahmin and all his followers are filled with joy and delight! We have come to offer you honour and reverence here at your feet.' (1028)

54 'May Bāvari the brahmin and all his followers be happy', said the Master. 'May you too be happy, young man, and may your life be long! (1029)

55 For Bāvari, for you and for all of your group there are many different doubts and confusions. You now have the opportunity to ask about them. Ask now whatever you want to know.' (1030)

56 The Man of Full Enlightenment had given Ajita permission. So the brahmin student respectfully sat down, made the folded-hand gesture, and addressed his first question to the Thus-Gone [Tathāgata]. (1031)

1. AJITA'S QUESTIONS

1 'What is it', said Ajita, 'that smothers the world? What makes the world so hard to see? What would you say pollutes the world, and what threatens it most?' (1032)

2 'It is ignorance which smothers', said the Master, 'and it is carelessness and greed which make the world invisible. The hunger of desire pollutes the world, and the great source of fear is the pain of suffering.' (1033)

3 'In every direction', said Ajita, 'the rivers of desire are running. How can we dam them and what will hold them back? What can we use to close the flood-gates?' (1034)

4 'Any river can be stopped with the dam of mindfulness', said the Buddha, 'I call it the flood-stopper. And with wisdom you can close the flood-gates.' (1035)

5 'Sir', said Ajita, 'where there is wisdom and mindfulness there is also the hybrid of mind and matter [the generation of individuality]. What brings it all to a halt?' (1036)

6 'This is the answer to your question, Ajita', said the Master. 'Individuality can be brought to a total end by the cessation of consciousness.' (1037)

7 'Sir', said Ajita, 'there are people here who have mastered all the teachings, and there are students and apprentices, and ordinary people too. Tell me how these people should live and work.' (1038)

8 'Let them be like a wanderer, a monk', said the Buddha. 'Mindful and skilful in everyway, they should free themselves from pleasure-hunger and make their minds [calm and] undisturbed.' (1039)

2. TISSA-METTEYYA'S QUESTIONS

Then the brahmin student Tissa-Metteyya asked the Master some questions:

1 'Who in the world is happy?' he asked.

'Is there anyone who isn't full of agitation?

'Is there anyone who can understand the alternatives without getting stuck in his thinking between them?

And who would you say deserved the title "superbeing"?

Who is there who isn't caught up in the patchwork world of greed?' (1040)

2 'There is a person who is not full of agitation', answered the Buddha.

It is the monk whose actions, in a sensuous world, are pure and good. He does not have the thirst of craving, he never loses mindfulness, and he has, by his own decision, become extinguished, calm. (1041)

3 He understands the alternatives without being stuck in the thinking between them. This is whom I would call a superbeing: a man beyond the patchwork world of greed.' (1042)

3. PUṆṆAKA'S QUESTIONS

The brahmin student Puṇṇaka was the next to speak:

1 'I have come', he said, 'to ask a question of the one without desire, the one with root-depth vision. It is this, Master, that I would like you to explain: why is it that the wise men in the world, the brahmins, the rulers and others, have always offered sacrifices to the gods?' (1043)

2 'These men', said the Buddha, 'were always making offerings to gods because, as they grew older, they wanted to preserve their lives as they were.' (1044)

3 'But, Master', said Puṇṇaka, 'did they ever get beyond old age and birth by making all these careful offerings?' (1045)

4 'Their prayers', said the Buddha, 'their praises, their offerings and aspirations were all made on a basis of possession, of reward: they longed for sensual pleasure. These men, these experts in offering, were delighting in the passion for becoming. These men could not go beyond getting old and being born.' (1046)

5 'You must explain this to me, Master', said Puṇṇaka. 'If all the offerings of the experts couldn't get them beyond ageing and birth, then who of all men, who of all the gods has ever managed to go beyond?' (1047)

6 'When a person has assessed the world from top to bottom', the Master said, 'when there is nothing in the world that raises a flicker of agitation, then he has become a person free from the smoke-fumes, the tremblings and the hunger of desire. He has become calm. He has gone beyond getting old; he has gone beyond being born.' (1048)

4. METTAGŪ'S QUESTIONS

Then the brahmin student Mettagū asked his question:

1 'Master', he said, 'you are clearly a mind of full development and a master of knowledge. Where on earth do all the different kinds of suffering come from?' (1049)

2 'This is a question', said the Master, 'about the birth and growth of suffering. I will answer it in the way that I myself have found it, which is this: all the different forms of suffering develop from the basic clinging. (1050)

3 When a person does not realize this he makes the basic attachment, the sluggish mind will undergo suffering. When a person realizes this he should not make the basic attachment seeing where suffering starts and grows.' (1051)

4 'That clearly answers what I asked, Sir', said Mettagū. 'Please answer this one too for me because of your certain knowledge. How do wise men cross the ocean? How can they get beyond the ageing process? How can they get beyond birth? or sadness? or sorrow?' (1052)

5 The Master replied: 'I will explain to you the truth, not based on hearsay. First, realize that this Way is one which can be known here and now, as a result of which a mindfully-living person releases his hold on the world.' (1053)

6 'Master Teacher', Mettagū said, 'for me there can only be joy and delight to hear you talk about a supreme Way which when a mindfully-living person knows it releases his hold on the world!' (1054)

7 The Master continued: 'In every direction there are things you know and recognize, above, below, around and within. Leave them: do not look to them for rest or relief, do not let consciousness dwell on the products of existence, on things that come and go. (1055)

8 This is how the wandering monk lives. He goes from place to place mindful and resolute. He does without cherished objects and comes to understand the world. So he leaves ageing and birth behind; he leaves sadness and sorrow behind; and he lets go of suffering here itself.' (1056)

9 'These great words of wisdom are full of joy for me', said Mettagū. 'Gotama's description of non-attachment is perfect. This master clearly has let go of suffering: he has found and understood just as it is the Way things work. (1057)

10 The people whom you, the Wisdom Master, regularly teach will certainly lose suffering. As for me, I have come here to honour you, to bow down before you, a hero. I ask you, Master, to give me frequent teachings.' (1058)

11 The Master answered: 'When you are aware that a man is a brahmin, a master of knowledge, a person with nothing, a creature with no ties to being or to pleasure, then, Mettagū, you have found an ocean-crosser, a traveller beyond the deserts and the doubts, a voyager who has reached the other shore. (1059)

12 This is a knower, a master of knowledge, a hero who has dissipated the pull of constant becoming, a man who has lost the clinging, the trembling and the hunger of desire. This, I would say, is the man who has gone beyond getting old; he has gone beyond being born.' (1060)

5. DHOTAKA'S QUESTIONS

The brahmin student Dhotaka was the next to speak:

1 'Master', he said, 'I so much want to hear you speak. Please, Master Teacher, explain to me: can a student of your teachings find the calm of cessation [Nibbāna] for himself?' (1061)

2 'Any student of my teaching', said the Buddha, 'who is eager, intelligent and aware, here and now, can find the calm of cessation for himself.' (1062)

3 'I can see now', said Dhotaka, 'that there is, in this world, a man who has nothing, a brahmin, a wanderer. I bow down and honour you, Sir, the eye that sees everything. Please, Man of Sākya, free me from confusion!' (1063)

4 'It is not in my practise to free anyone from confusion', said the Buddha. 'When you have understood the most valuable teachings, then you yourself will cross this ocean'. (1064)

5 'Have pity on me, brahmin, Sir', said Dhotaka. 'Please teach me the way of detachment, so that I can know it as it is, so that I can live, in this life, in the peace and independence that is as free as the air in space.' (1065)

6 'I will explain that peace which is not based on hearsay and is attainable here and now. It is a peace which, when a mindful person understands it, releases his hold on the world.' (1066)

7 'Master Teacher', said Dhotaka, 'it can only bring me joy to hear about an ultimate peace which, when a mindful person understands it, releases his hold on the world.' (1067)

8 'In every direction', said the Buddha, 'above, below, around and within there are things you know and recognize. When you realize that these are the things which tie you to the world, then you can lose the thirst of craving, the desire for constant becomings.' (1068)

6. UPASĪVA'S QUESTIONS

Then the brahmin student Upasīva asked a question:

1 'Man of Sākya', he said, 'it is not possible for me to cross the massive ocean alone and without help. You are the eye that sees everything; please tell me what I can use to help me across the ocean.' (1069)

2 The Master told Upasīva: 'Use these two things to help you cross the ocean: the perception of Nothingness[1] and the awareness that "there is nothing". Give up sense pleasures and be free from doubts so you will begin to see and to long for an end to craving.' (1070)

3 'Master', said Upsavīva, 'When a man is free from attachment to all pleasures and depends on nothingness, and everything else he lets go, he is freed in the supreme freedom from perception. But will he permanently be there and not return again?' (1071)

4 'When a man is free', said the Buddha, 'from all sense pleasures and depends on nothingness he is free in the supreme freedom from perception. He will stay there and not return again.' (1072)

5 'Master, you have the eye that sees everything', said Upasīva, 'If this man stays many years in this state without returning, will be cooled and freed there itself, say whether consciousness will still exist for such a person'. (1073)

6 'It is like a flame struck by a sudden gust of wind', said the Buddha. 'In a flash it has gone out and nothing more can be known about it. It is the same with a wise man freed from mental existence: in a flash he has gone out and nothing more can be known about him.' (1074)

7 'Please explain this clearly to me, Sir', said Upasīva. 'You, a wise man, know precisely the way these things work: has the man disappeared, does he simply not exist, or is he in some state of perpetual well-being?' (1075)

8 'When a person has gone out, then there is nothing by which you can measure him. That by which he can be talked about is no longer there for him; you cannot say that he does not exist. When all ways of being, all phenomena are removed, then all ways of description have also been removed.' (1076)

Note

1 Third Formless-sphere consciousness (*Arūpajjhāna*) which is taken by the yogi concentrating on it as *Natthi kiñci*, 'There is nothing whatever'.

7. NANDA'S QUESTIONS

The next of the brahmin students to speak was Nanda. This is what he asked the Buddha:

1 'Many people', he said, 'talk of Wise Men who, they say, are living in the world. What do you think about this? When they call someone "wise" are they talking about his knowledge or about the way he lives?' (1077)

2 'To the experts', said the Master, 'the word "wise" has nothing to do with the way a person sees things, or with what he has been taught, or with what he understands. To me, Nanda, a wise man is one who has disarmed: he lives in seclusion, without the tremble or the hunger of desire.' (1078)

3 'Then, Master', said Nanda, 'there is another question I must ask you. All religious teachers and brahmins have talked about the way to be pure. Some have said that purity comes from world-views and from teachings; some have said it comes from good deeds and religious rituals; others have said it comes from other things. Would you say, Sir, that these men, living in this world, who've taught these things, have gone beyond birth and ageing?' (1079)

4 'I would say this about religious leaders who teach that views and teachings, or deeds and rituals, or anything else will make you pure; I would say that these men, living in this world, have not gone beyond birth and ageing.' (1080)

5 'But Master', said Nanda, 'these men who teach that purity comes from views and teachings, or deeds and rituals and other things, these men are religious leaders, and you say that they are not ocean-crossers. I must ask you another question Sir: Can you, a Wise Man, say who in the world *has* gone beyond birth and ageing?' (1081)

6 'I do not say that all religious teachers and brahmins are wrapped in the shroud of birth and ageing', said the Buddha. 'There are some who have let go of world-views, of teaching traditions of thoughts. They have let go of religious practices and rituals, they have left all the different forms behind and they have a total understanding of attachments. For them there are no inner poison-drives. These, truly, are the ocean-crossers.' (1082)

7 'How perfect is the Wisdom Master's explanation of non-attachment!' said Nanda. 'It fills me with joy to hear it, and to hear that there are people who have let go of views, of traditions of thoughts; of religious practices and rituals; and of all the different forms. And these people have a total understanding of attachment — they have lost the inner poison-drives! These are the people whom I too will call the ocean-crossers!' (1083)

8. HEMAKA'S QUESTION

Hemaka was the next to speak:

1 'Before Gotama began to teach', he said, 'all teachings I had heard had only said, "This is how things used to be" and "This is how they're going to be?" Everything was based on tradition and hearsay which just increased my doubts. (1084)

2 So please now, Wisdom Master, explain to me the way you teach to put an end to craving. Explain to me the way you teach which, when a mindful-living person knows it, releases his hold on the world.' (1085)

3 'The removal of desire and passion for pleasant things, seen, heard or cognized is the sure path for the realization of Nibbāna. (1086)

4 Understanding this, those who are mindful have attained this tranquillity of complete Nibbāna in this immediate life. They are calmed for ever. They have crossed the attachment in this world.' (1087)

9. TODEYYA'S QUESTIONS

The brahmin student Todeyya spoke next:

1 'What, Sir, is the nature of freedom?', he questioned the Master, 'when one has no more desire for pleasure, goes beyond doubt and lives without craving?' (1088)

2 'A person who has no desires', said the Buddha, 'who has gone beyond doubt and who lives without craving, has indeed found the final freedom. For him there is nothing more to be freed.' (1089)

3 'All-seeing Sākyan', said Todeyya, 'please explain one other thing to me. I want to know how to recognize a wise man when I see him. Does the wise man still have any desires or is he completely wishless? Does he still need to learn or is his wisdom complete?' (1090)

4 'A wise man, Todeyya', said the Buddha, 'does not have desires, nor does he need to learn. He is wishless, he has wisdom, and you can recognize him because he is a man of nothing: he is not hanging on to pleasure or to being.' (1091)

10. KAPPA'S QUESTION

Next was the brahmin student Kappa:

1 'Sir', he said, 'there are people stuck midstream in the terror and the fear of the rush of the river of being, and death and decay overwhelm them. For their sakes, Sir, tell me where to find an island, tell me where there is solid ground beyond the reach of all this pain.' (1092)

2 'Kappa', said the Master, 'for the sake of those people stuck in the middle of the river of being, overwhelmed by death and decay, I will tell you where to find solid ground. (1093)

3 There is an island, an island which you cannot go beyond. It is a place of nothingness, a place of non-possession and of non-attachment. It is the total end of death and decay, and this is why I call it Nibbāna [the extinguished, the cool]. (1094)

4 There are people who, in mindfulness, have realized this and are completely cooled here and now. They do not become slaves working for Māra, for Death; they cannot fall into his power.' (1095)

11. JATUKAṆṆĪ'S QUESTION

Then the brahmin student Jatukaṇṇī spoke:

1 'I had heard', he said, 'that there was an ocean-crosser, a hero, desiring the desireless. And so I have come to ask a question of this man without desire. Tell me this, eye of instant seeing-knowing: what is the state of peace? Please explain it to me as it really is. (1096)

2 You, Master, rule desire and pleasure like the sun, with heat and light, rules and controls the earth. I have only a little understanding, Sir, and you are a globe full of wisdom. Tell me how to find and know the Way of giving up this world of births and ageings.' (1097)

The Buddha replied to Jatukaṇṇī:

3 'Lose the greed for pleasure. See how letting go of the world is peacefulness. There is nothing that you need hold on to and there is nothing that you need push away. (1098)

4 Dry up the remains of your past and have nothing for your future. If you do not cling to the present then you can go from place to place in peace. (1099)

5 There is a greed that fixes on the individual body-mind. When that greed has completely gone, then, brahmin, there will be no more inner poison-drives, without which you are immune from death.' (1100)

12. BHADRĀVUDHA'S QUESTION

The student brahmin Bhadrāvudha spoke next:

1 'I have come, he said, 'to ask a question. Thirst-breaker, wishless, free and wise, beyond time and home — life and pleasure — please, ocean-crosser, (1101)

2 for all the different people here who have come from different places to listen to your words. Tell us about the way that you have found and known.' (1102)

The Master replied:

3 'There is, in taking things, a thirst, a clinging, a grasping. You must lose it. You must lose it altogether, above, below, around and within. It makes no difference what it is you are grasping at: when a man grasps, Māra stands beside him. (1103)

4 Therefore, the monks, realizing this should not grasp at anything, being mindful. He should see the beings that are creatures of attachment as tied to the power of death.' (1104)

13. UDAYA'S QUESTIONS

Then the brahmin student Udaya spoke:

1 'Gone beyond in every way', he said, 'the ultimate in everything. When he sits in meditation there is no poison to infect him, no dust speck to impede him: He has done what has to be done.

[This is the man I have come to with my question, and this, Sir, is it:] Can you tell me about the knowledge that frees? Can you tell me how to remove ignorance?' (1105)

2 'The removal of both the intense desire for sensuous things,' said the Buddha, 'and the grief, the rejection of laziness and the resistance to worry'. (1106)

3 The purity of perfect, balanced mindfulness, built on a basis of seeing the Way Things Are: this is liberation-knowledge and this is the destruction of ignorance.' (1107)

[Udaya asked another question:]

4 'What binds and ties down the world? What causes the wandering? What is it that you abandon in order to find Nibbāna?' (1108)

5 'That which ties you down', said the Buddha, 'is the desire for pleasure. The wandering is applied thought. And the way to Nibbāna is to abandon the thirst of desire.' (1109)

6 'I have come with these questions, Master, and I hope you will answer one more', said Udaya. 'How does the mindful wanderer bring his mind-flow to an end?' (1110)

7 The Master replied: 'The sensations that he feels from the inside have no more fascination for him. And the sensations that he feels from the outside no longer fascinate. The wanderer is mindful and brings his mind-flow to an end.' (1111)

14. POSĀLA'S QUESTION

Then the student, Posāla, got up to speak:

1 'In everything', he said to the Master, 'you have reached perfection. There is not a movement of desire nor a remnant of doubt left in you. And so I have come to you, who can explain what has happened in the past, to ask this question. (1112)

2 I want to ask you, Man of Sākya, about knowledge. If a man is no longer confined to seeing forms, if he has discarded materialist limitations and he sees that there is neither inner nor outer substance to things, is there then anything more for him to know?' (1113)

3 'To the Tathāgata, the man-thus-come', replied the Buddha, 'all the aspects and stages of mind are clear. And so, when a person who has set his sights on freedom reaches his goal, the Tathāgata knows what stage he has reached. (1114)

4 When he has realized that the binding power of pleasure is rooted in nothingness, then he has come to a clear understanding of this process. This knowledge he, the completely accomplished brahmin, has achieved completely.' (1115)

15. MOGHARĀJA'S QUESTION

The next to speak was the brahmin student Mogharāja:

1 'Man of Sākya', he said, 'I have asked about this twice before without receiving an answer from the Wisdom-Eye. But I have heard that if a wisdom-god is asked a third time, then, he will give an answer. (1116)

2 I do not know, famous Gotama, what attitude you take towards this world and towards the other world, the world of Brāhma and the gods. (1117)

3 So, because of your insight into excellence, I have come to ask you about this. What is the best way for a person to regard the world so that the King of Death won't see him?' (1118)

The Master replied:

4 'If you are always aware, Mogharāja, you will look at the world and see its emptiness. If you give up looking at yourself as a soul [as a fixed and special identity], then you will have given yourself a way to go beyond death. Look at the world like this and the King of Death will not see you.' (1119)

16. PINGIYA'S QUESTION

Then the brahmin Piṅgiya spoke:

1 'I am old and decaying. My body is weak and my skin is pale. I can hardly see and I only hear with difficulty. Don't let me die while I am still in confusion but teach me about the Way Things Are so that I shall know how to leave birth and ageing behind me.' (1120)

2 'Look', replied the Buddha, 'look how many people are tormented by pain. Look how careless they are, and how greatly they suffer, because of body and forms. If you do not want to go on and on becoming, Piṅgiya, you must let go of the body and of forms.' (1121)

3 'In all the ten directions', said Piṅgiya, 'above, below, and in every quarter of the compass, there is not a thing that you have not heard, seen, known, or understood. Teach me about the Way Things Are so that I shall know how to leave birth and ageing behind me.' (1122)

4 'Can you see', replied the Buddha, 'how people are oppressed by desire? Can you see how they are racked and worn by ageing? If you do not want to go on and on becoming, Piṅgiya, you must let go of craving.' (1123)

PĀRĀYANA THUTI GĀTHĀ

(Epilogue)

This is what the Master said when the sixteen brahmins came to the Rock Temple in Magadha to ask him to answer their questions.

If you know what each question means, see what each question implies and live in accordance with the Way Things Are then you will go beyond. You will cross the ocean of death and ageing and reach the other shore.

These things lead to that other shore. That is why this teaching is called *Pārāyana* — 'The Way to the Beyond'.

1 There were sixteen of them who came to see the Buddha that time. There was Ajita, Tissa-Metteyya, Puṇṇaka, Mettagū, Dhotaka, Upasīva, Nanda and Hemaka; (1124)

2 Todeyya, Kappa and Jatukaṇṇī the scholar; Bhadrāvudha, Udaya, Posāla, Mogharāja the learned, and the great Piṅgiya the wise. (1125)

3 These were the men who came to see the Buddha, the man of perfect action. They came to the Buddha to put their complex questions to this paragon of understanding. (1126)

4 The Buddha answered the questions with the exactness of truth, just as things are; the brahmins were pleased to hear the words of this wise man. (1127)

5 And so, filled with pleasure by the clear-sighted vision of this Kinsman of the Sun,[1] they settled down to a life of purity and goodness spent in the shelter of the precious wisdom of the Buddha. (1128)

6 Anyone whose life accords with what the Buddha taught in these answers goes across the ocean. From here to the beyond, (1129)

7 from this shore to the other: this is crossing the ocean, this is travelling on the highest path. It is a path that leads to that other shore; that is why it is called *Pārāyana* — 'The Way to the Beyond'. (1130)

Piṅgiya's Praises of The Way to the Beyond

8 'I will sing you the praises of The Way to the Beyond', said Piṅgiya (when he returned to where the brahmin Bāvari lives on the banks of the River Godhāvari). 'It was described to us by this man exactly as he saw it. But then, there isn't any reason why a man like him should lie — a mammoth of knowledge and completely pure, a man without desire. (1131)

9 When a voice has none of the glibness of pride and none of the ingrained stains of ignorance, then its words are full of sweetness and beauty. It is such words that I praise now. (1132)

10 They call him Buddha, Enlightened, Awake, dissolving darkness, with total vision, and knowing the world to its ends, he has gone beyond all the states of being and of becoming. He has no inner poison-drives: he is the total elimination of suffering. This man, brahmin Bāvari, is the man I follow. (1133)

11 It is like a bird that leaves the bushes of the scrubland and flies to the fruit trees of the forest. I too have left the bleary half-light of opinions; like a swan I have reached a great lake. (1134)

12 Up till now, before I heard Gotama's teaching, people had always told me this: "This is how it has always been, and this is how it will always be"; only the constant refrain of tradition, a breeding ground for speculation. (1135)

13 This prince, this beam of light, Gotama, was the only one who dissolved the darkness. This man Gotama is a universe of wisdom and a world of understanding, (1136)

14 a teacher whose Dhamma is the Way Things Are, instant, immediate and visible all around, eroding desire without harmful side-effects, with nothing else quite like it anywhere in the world.' (1137)

15 'But Piṅgiya', said Bāvari, 'why then don't you spend all your time, your every moment, with this man Gotama, this universe of wisdom, this world of understanding, (1138)

16 this teacher whose Dhamma is the Way Things Are, instant, immediate and visible all around, eroding desire without harmful side-effects, and with nothing else quite like it anywhere in the world?' (1139)

17 'Brahmin, Sir', said Piṅgiya, 'there is no moment for me, however small, that is spent away from Gotama, from this universe of wisdom, this world of understanding, (1140)

18 this teacher whose teaching is the Way Things Are, instant, immediate and visible all around, eroding desire without harmful side effects, with nothing else quite like it anywhere in the world.' (1141)

19 'You see, Sir', said Piṅgiya, 'with constant and careful vigilance it is possible for me to see him with my mind as clearly as with my eyes, in night as well as day. And since I spend my nights revering him, there is not, to my mind, a single moment spent away from him. (1142)

20 I cannot now move away from the teaching of Gotama: the powers of confidence and joy, of intellect and awareness, hold me there. Whichever way this universe of wisdom goes it draws me with it. (1143)

21 Physically, I cannot move like that — my body is decaying, I am old and weak — but the driving power of purposeful thought propels me with it without break. (1144)

22 There was a time when, writhing in the mud of the swamps, I could only drift from one stone to the next. But then I saw the Sambuddha, fully awake and free from defilement.' (1145)

Then the Buddha spoke:

23 'Piṅgiya', he said, 'other people have freed themselves by the power of confidence. Vakkali, Bhadrāvudha and Āḷavi-Gotama have all done this. You too should let that strength release you; you too will go to the further shore, beyond the draw of death.' (1146)

24 'These words', said Piṅgiya, 'are the words of a man of wisdom. As I hear them I become more confident. This man is

Sambuddha: he has opened the curtains and woken up. There is nothing barren there; his mind is clear and luminous. (1147)

25 Everything accessible to knowledge is known to him, even the ultimate subtleties of godhood. There are no more questions for the doubtful who come to him: the teacher has answered them all. (1148)

26 Yes, I shall go there. I shall go beyond change, I shall go beyond formations; I shall go beyond comparison. There are no more doubts. You may consider this as mind released.' (1149)

Note

1 *Ādicca*. This appellation has been used synonymously for the more frequent word *suriya*. The Buddha is sometimes styled the Kinsman of the Sun (*ādiccabandhu*).

BIBLIOGRAPHY

Apart from complete translations in German, Italian and Swedish, together with individual *suttas* to be found in Asian and Western Buddhist magazines, the following complete translations and anthologies have been published in English:

E.W. Adikaram, *The Adventure and Struggle of the Buddha* [III 1 and 2] Wellampitiya [Sri Lanka] 1947

G.F. Allen, *Aṭṭhaka* [vagga] Bambalapitiya [Sri Lanka] 1958

——— *The Buddha's Philosophy* [I 3,12; III 8,11; IV 1 – 16; V 1 – 16] London 1959. [IV 2 repr. in John Walters *Mind Unshaken*, London 1961, repr. 1975, and, as *The Essence of Buddhism*, New York 1964]

Ananda Metteyya, *The Mahāmaṅgala and Vasala Suttas*. Colombo 1909

E.W. Burlingame, *Buddhist Parables* [I 2 and III 10] Yale University 1922

Lord [Robert] Chalmers, *Buddha's Teachings*. Cambridge, Mass. 1932

Edward Conze, *Buddhist Scriptures* [I 3; IV 16] Harmondsworth 1959, repr. 1983

Sir Muthu Coomaraswamy, *Dialogues and Discourses of Gotama Buddha* [I, II, III 7 – 9 and IV 1] London 1874. [I 1 – 3 repr. in Charles F. Horne (ed.) *The Sacred Books and Early Literature of the East* X (New York 1917), I 2,6,7,10; II 2,3,10; III 8,9; IV 1 in N. Ramesan *Glimpses of Buddhism* (Hyderabad 1961) and I 3 in Lucien Stryk (ed.) *World of the Buddha* (New York 1968, repr. 1982)]

Alexandra David-Neel, *Buddhism: its doctrines and its methods* [I 7 and II 4] London 1939, repr. 1977

Dharmakīrti Śrī Mirisse Indaratana, *Ratana Sutta*. Colombo 1978

V. Fausbøll, *A Collection of Discourses*. Oxford 1880; repr. Delhi 1973

D.J. Gogerly, tr. I 6,8 and II 1,4 for *The Friend* (Colombo 1839) repr. in the *Ceylon Friend* (Colombo 1880) and *Ceylon Buddhism* II (London 1908)

James Gray, *Mahāmaṅgala Sutta*. London 1892

E.M. Hare, *Woven Cadences of Early Buddhists*. London 1945, repr. 1947. [II 11 repr. in *Advice to Rāhula*, Kandy 1961, repr. 1974]

John D. Ireland, *The Discourse Collection* [II 3,6,8 – 11,14; III 2,8,12; IV 4 – 6,11,15; V 1,3,4,15,16] Kandy 1965

Mom Chao Upalisan Jumbala (tr. from Thai), *The Soḷasapañhā* [Pārāyaṇavagga] Bangkok 1956

Ria Kloppenborg, *The Paccekabuddha* [I 3 and its Commentary] Leiden 1974. Abridged ed., Kandy 1983

Mahasi (Sayadaw), *A Discourse on Hemavata Sutta*. Rangoon 1980

David Maurice, *The Lion's Roar* [I 8; II 2,4] London 1962; repr. New York 1967

Ñāṇamoli, *The Life of the Buddha* [I 4,8; III 1,2] Kandy 1973, repr. 1978. [All repr. in *The Buddha's Words* (Bangkok 1975) ed. Phra Khantipālo who tr. IV 5]

Nārada (Mahāthera), *The Light of the Dhamma* [I 6,8; II 1,4,10,14] Colombo 1939; repr. Singapore N.D.

——— *Vasala and Parābhava Sutta*. Colombo 1941

——— *A Manual of Buddhism* [I 6,8; II 4] Colombo 1949; repr. Kuala Lumpur 1971

——— *Everyman's Ethics* [I 6; II 4] Kandy 1959, repr. 1979

K.R. Norman, *The Group of Discourses* (with alternative translations by I.B. Horner and Walpola Rahula). Pali Text Society, London 1984

Nyanaponika, *The Worn-Out Skin* [= I 1] Kandy 1977

Nyanasatta, *Basic Tenets of Buddhism* [I 8; II 4] Colombo 1965

C. Paññālaṅkara, *Buddhism*. A Text-Book for S.S.C. Students [I 6] Colombo 1948, repr. 1949. [Repr. in Luang Suriyabongs *A Buddhist Anthology*, Bangkok 1957]

Ampitiye Rāhula, *Parābhava Sutta*. Colombo 1958

Walpola Rāhula, *What the Buddha Taught* [I 8; II 4] Bedford-London 1959, repr. 1982, and New York 1962

T.W. Rhys Davids, *The History and Literature of Buddhism* [I 2; II 10; III 1] London 1896; repr. Calcutta 1962. [III 1 repr. in T.W. Rhys Davids *Early Buddhism* (London 1914) and Lucien Stryk (ed.) *World of the Buddha* (New York 1968, repr. 1982)]

H. Saddhātissa, *The Buddha's Way* [I 6; II 4,14] London 1971

D.M. Strong, *The Metaphysic of Christianity and Buddhism* [I 2; III 1] London 1899

Anagārika P. Sugatānanda [Francis Story] (ed.), *Saṅgīti* [I 2; II 4] Rangoon 1954. [II 4 repr. in John Walters *Mind Unshaken*, op. cit.]

E.J. Thomas, *Early Buddhist Scriptures* [II 4; III 1; V 6] London 1935

——— *The Road to Nirvāṇa* [I 2; II 1] London 1950

Sister Vajirā, *Sutta Nipāta* I Uragavagga. Sarnath 1941. II Cūlavagga. Sarnath 1942

[I 8; II 1,4 adapted by H. Saddhātissa as *Three Suttas for Daily Recitation*, Sarnath 1956]

See also the following analytical, descriptive or exegetical works:

G.F. Allen, *The Buddha's Philosophy*. London 1959, pp. 73 – 82.

Grace Gayle Burford, 'The Ideal Goal according to the Aṭṭhakavaga and its major Pali Commentaries'. Ph.D. diss., Northwestern Univ., Evanston 1983.

N.A. Jayawickrama, 'A critical analysis of the Pali Sutta Nipāta illustrating its gradual growth'. Ph.D. diss., London Univ. 1947. Published in serial form *Ceylon University Review* (1948 – 51) and *Pali Buddhist Review* (London 1976 – 8).

B.C. Law, *A History of Pali Literature* I. London 1933; repr. Delhi 1974, pp. 232 – 60.

K.R. Norman, *Pāli Literature*. Wiesbaden 1983, pp. 63 – 70.

G.C. Pande, *Studies in the Origins of Buddhism*. Univ. of Allahabad 1957; repr. Delhi 1974, pp. 51 – 65.

P.D. Premasiri, *The Philosophy of the Aṭṭhakavagga*. Kandy 1972

M. Winternitz, *History of Indian Literature* II. Univ. of Calcuta 1933; repr. New Delhi 1972, pp. 92 – 8.